THE FIRST TRUTH

A Book of Metaphysical Theories

Author: David Almeida

Library of Congress Control Number 2013900430

Printed in the United States of America.

Mystic River Publishing

First Edition

Acknowledgments

I would like to express my sincere appreciation to all those who have contributed to my happiness and to all those who helped make this book possible. This includes my wife, family, friends, editors, and readers. You are blessed with abundance and beauty.

Comments

The theories and ideas presented in this book were communicated to me through the spirit of Arthur Edward Waite, the famed occult scholar. I realize this statement may sound preposterous to some people. That is understandable. I have no problem with any skepticism and resistance to my assertions regarding this. I am confident that the majority of the people purchasing this book are open-minded and comfortable with the idea of spirit communication.

My knowledge of Waite is limited to a few Internet websites I consulted after discovering his presence in my life. An accounting of this matter is brought up later in the book. I understand that A.E. Waite is best known for the Waite tarot card deck, which was illustrated by Pamela Cole Smith during his involvement with the Hermetic Order of the Golden Dawn. However, Waite's greatest life contribution was to occult literature. Waite was an avowed mystic and author of several texts concerned with the occult sciences.

A.E. Waite's name meant nothing to me growing up (I was only familiar with his last name), despite the fact that my mother read tarot cards for entertainment. In fact, I am not particularly fond of the tarot deck and as of this printing; I have not read any of Waite's books. Recently I purchased a copy of Waite's *Complete Rosicrucian Initiations of the Fellowship of the Rosy Cross*. The back cover states that this book is the manual for the inner workings of his mystical order. I admit I found the writing in this book to be a bit challenging, and so I decided to set it aside for another time. My writing style is significantly different from Waite's, largely due to his being a British author of the late 19ᵗʰ and early 20ᵗʰ century.

From what I can gather, my personality is dissimilar from that of Waite. It seems Waite was highly regarded for his literary talent and not his character. To this day, mystical scholars despise Waite for the sarcastic and critical writings that have become part of his legacy. I do not suppose that this is the type of person that one would choose as a spirit guide. Assuming it is possible to choose one's guides. Nonetheless, I feel privileged to have this accomplished writer working on my behalf, if for nothing other than inspiration. One does not have to comprehend the size and value of another person's impact on the world to appreciate his apparent achievements. The mere presence of such a person conveys a sense of excellence that one must aspire to.

Table of Contents

Acknowledgments ....… 3
Comments ....….................................. 4
Table of Contents ….. 5
Introduction …... 6
Concepts...14
Reincarnation 20
Good and Evil 40
Perfection 48
On Certain Entities... 56
Drugs and Mental Illness 67
Dimensions of Reality 75
Universal Laws 100
Humans and the Multiverse... 142
Epilogue 188
About the Author 190

Introduction

I am only able to address certain aspects of life after death, since this subject is very broad. Speaking on the entire composition of the multiverse would be like trying to discuss every conceivable aspect of the living world (the term *multiverse* is used to describe the entire composition of the physical and nonphysical existences). Think of trying to explain the complex nature of this world to an uninformed stranger. What would you talk about? You could discuss economics, politics, entertainment, education, etc. But what else could you say? It's endless. The same holds true for the other side. Where do you begin and where do you end?

I have made the subject of this book the nature of reality, since its understanding is necessary to possess an understanding of the afterlife. This topic will become clear as you get deeper into the book. For the record, I will state that skeptics will win any argument against the validity of the information contained in this book, since it does not conform to the principles of modern science. However, it cannot be disproved either. The very idea of validating God is inconceivable through our limited view of the universe. That puts organized religion in a precarious position.

I am not trying to impress the skeptics. I do not need to put my time and energy into that pursuit. My hope is to enlighten those individuals who are willing to expand their awareness by exploring new ideas. There are many texts written on this subject. I am not interested in duplicating what they have done.

I will call this book a metaphysical work. There are no all-encompassing words available to describe the information conveyed within these pages. That would be a difficult task since we are dealing with the unknown. Please understand your reasoning skills will not help you comprehend this material. For my part, I will do my best to present this material in an understandable manner.

There are a few items I need to clarify regarding my writing style. Whenever possible, I will substitute popular yet overly used words and phrases in favor of expressions that are more suitable. Some of these misused terms include "astral world," "astral universe," "astral plane," "astral travel," "astral projection," and "astral energy." These terms tend to be used very broadly. I use them occasionally when there are no other terms to describe aspects of the non-physical dimensions. Some people like to use the word "astral" to describe the place in which we find ourselves immediately upon death. It has been said by some metaphysical writers that the astral world is divided into a number of planes. I do not have sufficient knowledge of this, but I will share some ideas of my own.

I also want to clarify my position on two key words used quite often throughout this text: "mind" and "consciousness." I find their definitions to be highly ambiguous. Some would argue that mind is a feature of consciousness, while others say consciousness is a manifestation of the mind. I am not aware of a separation between these two concepts. However, this could be the case. I have chosen to exchange one for another in different places for variety. There is no underlying reason for this.

Death is arguably the biggest mystery of them all. What lies beyond life has perplexed humankind from the very beginning. There have been numerous religions and philosophies built around this event. Each person has his or her own idea of what will happen after death. Of course, some people, namely atheists, believe it ends here. Most people have borrowed ideas about the afterlife from others. Typically, these beliefs are instilled in us when we are young, usually by our parents. Our parents got their beliefs from whatever religion was accepted in their community. I went to a Methodist church. Their position on the afterlife is that you go to heaven when you die. I never got a sense of what heaven is like. The church officials never talked about what heaven looked like or what you do there.

I have my own strong beliefs about life after death. This guide will present pieces of my theories, which you may choose to accept or reject. Chances are that you would not be reading this book if you were not open to new ideas. My theories come from a long study of metaphysics and time spent in meditation. I believe it would be far better for you to find your own way through this "spiritual" process, rather than simply to adopt what I have to say about it. Everyone has his or her own path to follow. Do not follow the same path I took; it may not get you to where you need to be. Use this book as a guide, not a step-by-step manual for illumination.

My experience with death started when I was a teenager. I know that many teens have what adults see as a preoccupation with death. Maybe they are depressed. Some are fascinated. Most are just curious. In my case, I wanted to know where I came from and where I will eventually end up. I guess it was a "calling." I didn't accept the idea of heaven, although now I know that the Christian heaven is one of the many places we may encounter on the other side, depending upon our expectations. Starting with my younger days, I have maintained a strong interest in what has become known as astral projection. This is a fully-fledged out-of-body experience (OOBE). I base my beliefs about the afterlife on reports provided by astral travelers, human contact with otherworldly entities, and my own intuitive insights.

I am selective about where I get my information. I am a natural skeptic. My trust is not easily won on such matters, and so I feel that my beliefs are solid. I must again admit that there is no way to validate any of the information on this subject. No one can agree on what constitutes the truth. This impasse leaves us with limiting beliefs that effectively distort whatever bit of truth any group chooses to claim as its own. No one can state otherwise. That's why there are so many religions and philosophies. It's easy to push one's spiritual beliefs on others when they are desperate for the truth.

Keep in mind that the truth I am speaking will not set you free. Yet, the truth will change your life; you will never see things the same way again. I suppose many religions also claim this. The truth will set you on your destined path. This does not mean you are an unwilling slave of the Universal Mind. You will want this job. It will become your way of life. The pursuit of higher knowledge in this world does not end until we have reached the end of our physical existence.

Having said this, I realize that for most people, the truth can be extremely frightening. As a general rule, people want to hide from the truth. They are afraid of what it will reveal about them. This statement should not make anyone feel inferior or hopeless. Shielding ourselves from the truth is part of the human condition. It's a protective measure of sorts. It becomes apparent in many areas of our lives. The truth doesn't always set you free in the usual way of thinking; sometimes it creates a myriad of challenges that we must overcome. My personal metaphysical investigations have led me to believe that at this stage in our development, our shared reality would no longer function if the big picture unfolded before us. If the population knew the ultimate truth, the Master Plan would fail. I believe that the forces that created this reality decided that we should come into the world with amnesia, so as not to put a monkey wrench into the Grand Scheme. If we knew the meaning of life, we would have no incentive to participate. Total awareness of our situation would defeat the purpose. If you could know your future without a hint of doubt, including the bad stuff, how would that affect you? Would you try to avoid these events? Trust me, that would make things worse. When we have all claimed our illumination, our circumstances will change for the better. That day is coming.

It's clear to me that protection from the truth is in our best interest – at least for the time being. Having said that, I am going to change my tune and declare that some higher knowledge of our earthly existence is incredibly helpful to our spiritual evolution. Almost every religion and philosophy in our past and in the present day has received some part of the Master Plan. Does that mean every religion is "right"? At least partially so. It seems as if the Creator only gives one piece of the puzzle at a time. Perhaps our esteemed benefactor only gives us what we can handle. Because the meaning of life is elusive, no one will ever know if their theories about death are correct until they have gone through it. However, since mankind has been on this planet for thousands of years, we have enough information to piece together a simple map for navigating through this human experience. We each have our own map, of course. I prefer GPS.

Now, seeing the truth is one thing, but understanding it is another. We see the truth all of the time. We usually ignore truth's manifestations and brush them off as hallucinations, accidents, coincidences, and even luck. That is not the case, for we have a god of order. Events are not random. The universe is incredibly organized. We know this by studying the universal laws, such as cause and effect. This world only has the appearance of chaos. I touch on this issue throughout this text, so there is no need to cover it here.

Most of us carry a fear of death. Fear is a common emotion in regards to death. Fear of death comes from our anxiety of confronting the unknown, as well as the fact that we will be facing it alone. The only reference we have for death is the knowledge of those who have gone before us. We are uncomfortable with this. The loss of a loved one can be difficult for anyone to accept. Some people become deeply disturbed at the passing of a family member or close friend. Few of us can say that death has no effect on them. Any death we witness can traumatize us. Our lives are never the same after experiencing another person's death. In a sense, death is our greatest teacher. Those attitudes and feelings that we display towards the death of another helps us to grow in ways that would not happen otherwise. Death changes us. We come to appreciate life more. Even when we grieve a loved one's passing for years, it is a valuable experience. There are lessons that emerge from these events. We may receive a new mission. Some parents of missing children have started new lives because of their loss. These brave couples and individuals have assumed leadership roles in non-profit organizations dedicated to child safety. I realize that no one wants to have this experience. Our losses speed up our personal growth process. Loss makes us examine our relationship or experience with the person that passed on.

The First Truth

Concepts

Walls

With regard to the Great Awakening awaiting us, a discussion is needed about the subject of walls. Walls serve many different purposes. Those of us who believe in an afterlife prefer a dualistic reality. The administrators of this reality have us believe in the here and there, or this side and the other side. We acknowledge the existence of materialism and spiritualism. Then we put up an imaginary wall separating the two. Some of you may remember The Doors song, "Break on Through to the Other Side," which debuted in the late 1960s. This song hints at breaking through some sort of "psychic" barrier, although its true meaning lies with Jim Morrison. Can you tell what generation I relate to?

Walls mean many things. In most cases, walls are more harmful than beneficial. They can be physical, mental, emotional, and spiritual. We use them for protection in an effort to keep people out. This serves both our physical and emotional needs. The problem is that walls are not discriminatory. They keep everyone out; even those who love us and give us support. They also keep us inside, isolated from the world. We cannot experience personal growth when we limit ourselves.

Any old walls you have built up over the years must be taken down in order to see the light of day. We accomplish this task one brick at a time. It took years to put up our walls, and it will take some time to tear them down. We cannot even begin this process until we recognize that our psychological or spiritual walls exist. The majority of us, absorbed with our own personal reality, fail to make this realization. When our walls finally come down, we sit in amazement. We experience a sense of freedom and

15

lightness. This happens when we discover our inner senses and open our minds to the truth.

Let's talk about the spiritual aspect of walls. Once again, we see a duality. This has to do with the law of polarity. I will be discussing the universal laws later, but for now, the universal duality I speak of manifests as the physical and the nonphysical. This can also be interpreted as heaven and Earth, material and spiritual, life and death, etc. There are many ways to describe this major duality. Because there are two sides to life, we assume there is a division. This is the brilliant illusion that we know as life and death. Since, under most circumstances, we can't experience what exists outside of this world, we imagine what it must look like. We believe there is another side, so we create religions and philosophies to understand it. We feel defeated at times, because of our limited ability to reach "God." We want to ''break through'' and see the truth.

Walls block our relationship with the Divine Source. The Divine is always communicating with us. However, our perception of a wall leaves us all but spiritually disconnected. Some walls represent our obsessive interest in the material aspects of the world. This intense focus on the material plane leaves us unaware that another world exists. We are reinforcing the notion that an imaginary wall keeps us from experiencing the truth. If we overindulge in the drama of our lives, we block out the love that the Infinite has for us. The loving collective consciousness that is God cannot get through to us. We may not even entertain the idea of a Supreme Being.

In a symbolic sense, some walls are made of stone. Stone walls are strong and are difficult to overcome. In this context, you may have heard the phrase "a hardened heart." Those familiar with the Old Testament will recall

God being unable to reach the hardened heart of Pharaoh. The Infinite reaches relatively few of us in the modern world. Many of us have become lost in the physical world, believing that there is nothing beyond what we see.

If there is a world outside of our own, then there must be an invisible barrier preventing us from seeing it. That is what we perceive to be the wall. The wall keeps our worlds separate. It's simple enough to say that the invisible wall doesn't exist, but nevertheless, the afterworld exists right before our eyes. If we could just take our eyes off of the material world for a moment, we would see extraordinary things. However, it's not our eyes that can sense the invisible world; it's our inner senses that perceive it. The Collective Consciousness gives us external senses and internal senses. The external senses consist of five recognized sensory modes: vision, hearing, smell, taste, and touch. The internal senses that allow us to access the unknown worlds consist of relatively little used tools such as imagination, dreams, visions, intuition, creativity, telepathic reception, and apprehension of divine knowledge. There are likely several other extrasensory tools I have not mentioned here. Some argue that astral projection should be included in this list.

When we flip a penny to make a decision, we say "heads or tails." Between those two sides is the middle. This area could also be considered a wall. In that line of thinking, a great duality exists between the internal and external. The uninformed refer to this as life and death. These opposing forces are but one and the same. Since the majority of you agree that there is no death, there can only be life. The law of polarity is truly an illusion of the physical world. The external and internal worlds are one. I have dubbed this illusion the "internal and external conflict." There is no separation between here and there. In fact, there is no "there." There exists only here and now. Yet, even though we are just experiencing the illusory sense of a divided reality, I will insist that these divisions are necessary and fundamental to our existence at this time. A wall does exist for our best interests, but it is only a virtual wall and does not exist in any real sense.

The First Truth

Reincarnation

Let's move on to the all-important concept of reincarnation. My feeling is that almost all religions and quasi-religious movements teach the continuation of the soul after death. Within this majority are a number of faiths that subscribe to the notion of reincarnation. Many of you are probably familiar with this principle. Reincarnation is a concept that is often associated with Hinduism. Buddhists also speak of it as "rebirth." I am most familiar with the Rosicrucian teachings on reincarnation. My own take on reincarnation starts with the idea that "God" has sent us here into this physical reality to experience life and bring those resulting experiences back to the source. I believe that God is learning. God is evolving and expanding with each new experience we contribute to it. We experience spiritual growth with each new incarnation. This is also true for God. You could say this is my interpretation of the meaning of life. It comes down to learning and growth.

This leads into a discussion on the perfection of our Greater Self, as well as that of the Infinite. The Divine Consciousness, as well as our own, is evolving and expanding. We are seeking new ways to improve. That is the universal mandate. We grow in understanding with each new incarnation. Since God does not know what it is like to be human (each life is unique), the opportunity exists for growth and development through physical existence. Each incarnation is unique. Therefore, each life provides new experiences to add to our Greater Self. This, in turn, allows the God of creation to climb the evolutionary ladder, taking on an entirely new form with each step. There appears to be no end to this cycle. I'm sorry to say that there is no prize awaiting us at some imagined finish line. This is truly the meaning of life. It's fairly uncomplicated and straightforward. We are here to learn and grow. Spir-

itual evolution, as I am describing it, is the most fundamental concept in this book.

We choose our lives based on our needs. It may be
that we may need to learn a lesson of some sort. In one
life, we may have had problems with money. In that case,
we may decide to spend our next life as a beggar. This is a
critical point. We chose much of our existence by setting
up tests and challenges. We are creative beings. We are
always trying new angles to test ourselves. If you have a
debilitating physical or emotional disorder, you may have
created this condition to challenge yourself. You may have
a serious illness such as Lupus. There could be several reasons why you chose this. You may have wanted to experience life with Lupus in order to gain new insights on what
it is like to have a debilitating illness. Perhaps you wanted
the challenge of overcoming this disease. Though your life
will be a painful one, the experiences you gain will be
worth it after you leave this world. That may or may not be
helpful. You might be surprised to know that persons with
severe intellectual disabilities have fabulous insight. A life
of hardship, or even destitution, has its experiential merits.
As I said, learning is a key ingredient to the meaning of
life. Formal education is not a requirement. You do not
need to worry if you were a high school dropout.

Of course, we are here to enjoy ourselves too. Entertainment is as essential as any serious venture. I don't
think we would come here if it were all work and no play.
We are pleasure-seeking beings. Our five senses can make
our lives enjoyable. It may be that we just want to indulge
ourselves in money, sex, and drugs. Vices can become the
sole reason for an incarnation. I'm sure we have all done
this in one of our many past lives.

We try to set the intention and general circumstances
of our new life. We usually choose where we are to be

born and to whom. We also like to arrange the significant events and the direction we are to follow. Even if we make these choices, life may sweep us up and take us in a different direction. Life has a way of interfering with our pre-life intentions. Things do not always go the way we plan. If we do get our way, it may not turn out to be the experience we wanted. You may decide to live the life of a rock star and discover its dark side. That may make the glamorous life less appealing than a modest existence.

The course of our life is subject to a number of external factors. Some of these factors include the law of attraction, the Cosmic Intelligence, our Greater Self, guides, and the presence of others in our personal reality. As you can see, our lives are subject to the influence of the many beings that have an interest in our spiritual growth. Sometimes we get what we want, and other times we get what our spirit helpers know is good for us.

We have free will in this reality. However, life is not random. Events are not subject to chance, accidents, and coincidences. We reside in a skillfully orchestrated universe. The inner workings are superb. There is no contradiction between free will and order. Both coexist rather well in this universe. Just as most societies have laws, the Cosmic Consciousness gives us freedom within certain parameters.

A number of different factors and forces determine the time of our passing. The most common reason is that it may simply be your time. We typically choose the time and circumstances of our death before we come into this world. Once we have accomplished our missions, we will depart this life, even if we believe it is not our time. Our ethereal self may have different plans.

Many of us wonder why God cuts a person down in his prime. The real reason is that we made these arrangements ourselves. These events arrive carefully planned and packaged. Even a young child dying of cancer has likely completed his or her mission. That mission may have been to teach his parents a valuable lesson. This difficult test was likely prearranged by several parties in between lives. I realize this may not be comforting to the grieving parents. I have seen this reality as a hospice volunteer.

Other reasons for an untimely death may be that your Greater Self, or even the Universal Consciousness, determined that one's mission is finished. This scenario is the equivalent of our belief that God decides the time of our death. Such an assertion takes the decision out of your hands. I am not sure how often this happens. Higher beings have their reasons for making such judgments. Divine intervention of this kind is always in our best interest. It also furthers the evolution of the Infinite Source.

In many cases, our deaths may be determined by consulting with guides and teachers during the sleep cycle. While you are sleeping, you are busy with your spirit classes. During this period, we are analyzing the previous day and making calculations for the events of the new day. There is considerable training involved. An eight-hour period of sleep is entirely different on the other side. A great deal can be accomplished in this amount of time. Our teachers help us decide what actions to take in our physical lives. We are all faced with possibilities. Each possibility claimed by us has enormous implications. Some of them become probabilities. Our teachers guide us through which probabilities are most beneficial to our evolution. This includes our deaths. Once again, death is our greatest teacher, especially when it comes to the death of others. We learn a valuable lesson from the death of our loved ones.

We can gain valuable insights from any death we witness, if we so choose. It might not be pleasant, but then again it would be a little morbid if you derived pleasure from someone's death.

Let me give you some of my own past and present life insights:

I believe that one of my objectives for reincarnating in this life was to be a detective. I guess I wanted to experience the excitement for myself. I learned the truth behind the inflated hype about having a detective's career. I discovered that it's an interesting profession, and at times it can be intriguing. However, it's only exciting in the very beginning. I'm probably one of those souls who crave action. Maybe next time I'll be a Navy SEAL.

Aside from this need to be on the edge, I have a strong pull in the direction of magic and mysticism. This has been a long-running theme through my reincarnational cycle. The group I choose to associate with in this life ascribes to a thought system that I have occupied myself with in previous lives. That may be why I seem to know their teachings even before I am given them. I have also received impressions during a shamanic journeying experience that I had been a member of the ancient mystery schools somewhere in northern Africa. That does not make me in any way special. Many people were mystics in those days. That was the higher education of the time.

It's fine to speculate about such things; just try to be careful of your judgments in this world. It is only life. We play all the roles. As we work on perfecting our being, we are also learning to perfect the world.

Life Review: A Reincarnational Self-Examination

Without a doubt, we all have room to improve. There are parts of us that are in need of an upgrade. Examining yourself is a lifelong process. It is especially important that you do this near the end of your life since you will have accumulated the majority of your experiences. Additionally, your perspective on your accumulated experiences will have changed by that point.

As a spiritual counselor, I cannot give answers. I can only ask questions, because you have all the answers. It doesn't do any good for me to try to counsel you on what you already know. The process of reflection may be a painful experience, but entirely necessary. Try not to judge yourself. What's done is done, and it's time to evaluate what you have learned from your experiences. You can start doing this at any point in your journey. It will contribute to your spiritual growth. Reflection will make you a better person in this life too. Try just fifteen minutes a day. The process of reflection shouldn't take you away from your daily activities. It should be a tool to help you improve your current life and prepare you for the next. Please don't get carried away with it.

Many people have no goals in mind when they decide to return to physical reality. Some individuals simply want to have the time of their life. Therefore, this reflection is of limited use to them. One of my inspirations this time around was to experience the "thrill of being a real-life private detective." I did that. As I said, the career was exciting at times, but the hassles made it unappealing.

The reflection process is not meant to scare you or make you feel bad about yourself. Neither is it meant to make you come out looking like a saint. Good and bad is nonexistent in this universe. To my mind, karma is a myth and does not exist. You will not be judged upon exiting this reality, nor will you have to pay for your transgressions in another life. It's probable that in your next incarnation you will work on improving your deficiencies. This is an opportunity, not a punishment.

I also want to point out that past lives retain their own distinct personalities. It's not just "you" in another life. These personalities are "you," but also separate from you. Have you ever heard someone talk about his or her younger self and say, "I was a different person then"? That's very true. Your earlier self was a different person. It's the same with your past lives. I know this is confusing. That's metaphysics. My own dark past life will serve as an example. Please read on.

At one time, I thought I was being punished for wrongdoings in a past life. Over the years, I have received simple communications from dark entities connected with the Golden Dawn. They may have been reaching out to me. Old demons have trouble letting go.

I've never taken part in a past life regression, but I have some idea about my previous incarnation. In the mid-1990s, I was sitting in front of my computer when I perceived a mental voice that spoke the name "Therion." This name did not mean anything to me at the time. I immediately looked it up on the Internet. I discovered that "Therion" is a magical name used by Aleister Crowley. Another incident came to me in the early summer of 2011, when I was meditating. The number 93 appeared in my mind. I realize numbers can have multiple meaning or no meaning at all. I have no experience with numerology or the meaning of numbers, so I proceeded to look it up. It turns out that 93 is the numerical representation of the Thelemic system (It certainly has several meanings). I have never had a strong interest in Crowley, and I know very little

27

about him. Months later, I attended a spiritualist church, where a medium served as the pastor. During a meditation circle, the pastor declared that Arthur was present for me. I didn't notice anything special about this five-minute session. I went home and called my parents to inquire about Arthur. I came up empty handed. I also went to checking genealogies on the internet. I saw an entry for an Arthur Edward on one website. Suddenly it came to me as if by divine inspiration – Arthur Edward Waite. I admit I was familiar with his name as a teenager from *The Book of Ceremonial Magic*, although I hadn't read it.

In a private session a week later, I asked the pastor if the spirit named Arthur is the 20th century occult writer and mystic Arthur E. Waite. She was silent for a moment and then said, "Does he go back and forth between good and bad?" I said yes, since I had looked him up.

On another occasion, a different medium received an image of an old-fashioned writing desk and a chair. I could only speculate as to what this meant. Months later, my wife saw this same desk and chair in a dream. The desk was situated in a space within our bedroom. Apparently, Arthur has assisted me in writing my books. He appeared to other mediums at the church several times to offer his support for my previous book *Illusion of the Body: Introducing the Body Alive Principle*. Although I have not read his books, I am grateful to have an accomplished writer on my side.

I know that even a modest skeptic will see all of this as nonsense, since I already knew the name A.E. Waite, but the way that information comes to you makes it right. It is only possible to explain this if you have experienced divine illumination.

I am familiar with the Waite deck. My mother read tarot cards for close to fifty years. The cards have piqued my interest at times, but I've never had a strong attachment to them. Although I do not know the works of A.E. Waite, throughout my life I have attached myself to the dark grimoires mentioned in *Ceremonial Magic*. I almost felt good having them. It gave me a sense of both peace and power. I would sell them or give them away from time to time, only to buy them back again. I am much more attracted to mysticism and Rosicrucian philosophy than to the black arts.

Early on, I had the impression that Arthur wasn't highly regarded in his time. I soon learned that Waite wasn't a likeable person by most people's measure. Occult enthusiasts have had nothing good to say about his character. Is he someone a person would choose for a past life? Possibly, but not based on his personality. Occultists and mystics credit Waite for his significant contributions to occult literature. I do not have a lot of interest in Waite's work. I have my own projects to put my energy into. Reincarnations are like that. My reincarnational speculations are open to criticism, since they are just observations made from the outside looking in. I'm comfortable with that.

Reincarnation Self-Examination Questions:

What is your mission(s)?

You can identify your missions with the major themes in your life. Look at your struggles (we have all struggled with something) and your passions. Struggles can include money, health, family, spiritual, and relationships among other things. Passion is a deep interest or intense love focused on a specific activity, object, or person. Most people recognize this in their vocation or avocation. At other times, the mission will pop up intermittently throughout your life. If you do your homework, you will see the patterns. They are unmistakable. With awareness of your missions, you can unlock powerful secrets. Your time in this world will count for so much more.

How do you feel about your life based on what you have done?

Based on your life experiences – at least the ones that come back to you clearly – how do you feel you did in completing your mission? If you do not know your missions at this point, you need to spend time thinking about this. If you cannot identify your mission for this life, then the next logical question would be: did you overcome each challenge you encountered along the way? Search yourself. Give yourself an honest assessment of what you took away from each event. Even if you feel that you failed yourself and others, did you learn a valuable lesson? That is what counts. These learning experiences will advance you spiritually. You will take this information with you into the next life to continue with the learning process.

Are there areas that you feel need improvement? If so, what are they?

I hope that there are lessons you have taken away from the tests you set up for yourself in this life. Try to pin down what it is you need to work on. We all have some areas that require further development in order to mature in spirit. This is true unless you have reached the end of your reincarnational cycle. Maybe some of your relationships with other people need work. Perhaps you would like to work on your relationship with money. A problematic relationship with money is indicative of an unhealthy attitude toward materialistic principles. It could be that you need to perfect your relationship with the Collective Consciousness. Your spiritual beliefs may not be where they should be.

As you can see, relationships play a most significant role in our lives. We cannot live or grow without them. There are many areas in our relationships in need of improvement. Only you know what they are. It may take a fair amount of contemplation to uncover the truth. However, even if your time is short, you should still have enough time to figure out the key pieces.

What can I take away from the significant events of my life?

Keep in mind that even the minor events can be valuable if they made a big impact on your life. You want to look specifically at what these events meant to you and how they changed you. Every event changes you to some degree, even if it isn't apparent. Ask yourself if anything from a particular event could help to motivate you in your pursuit of perfection. It can be frustrating to do this at first, but as you get going, the pieces will fall into place. Keep in mind that not every gem you pick up will come from a positive place. The same is true of the negative occurrences. Real life does not work that way. There is always the good in the bad and the bad in the good. There's something to learn from every experience.

Even a casual exchange at the bus stop holds enormous ramifications for your life. Some interactions mean more to us than others. The memorable ones are the experiences that seem to affect us the most. They tend to define us through our own interpretation of them. Our job is to interpret them in an impartial manner. We will continue to do this even when we transition to the other side. It never hurts to get an early start. Reflection is a life-long process. It's just that the end is especially important.

Did I successfully meet these tests according to my own perception of success? Am I being honest with myself about this?

At this stage, you should be determining if you successfully conquered those challenges that you set down for yourself before coming into this world. First, you must establish your criteria for determining what success would be for the particular episode you are considering. What would make this experience one from which you can walk away with confidence? Did your performance in this instance meet your standard of excellence? Realize that your standards are measured in your own way and are as valid as anyone else's. If you feel good about the situation, and you are comfortable that your actions were entirely appropriate for the situation, and then it is time to move on.

Is there something you would have done differently?

Did you meet each item in the challenges you recognize? Did these little victories lead to successful outcomes, or were there things that you wish you could redo? If you wish you could go back and fix parts of a particular event, is it possible that you still came out a winner? Is it something you can say was successful and does not need to be repeated? If you feel you have loose ends stemming from the incident, you should examine them and ask yourself how important they are in the scheme of things. Are they really worth the energy you are giving to them? If they were truly important, how would you envision a successful outcome for the individual episodes? What would you have said or done differently? This should be your interpretation of success, not someone else's. How would things change for the positive, in your amended scenario? Deep down, are you sure you understand what the outcome should have looked like? Try to visualize it in your mind. It may be difficult to do, but it's meant to help you move forward. By doing this, you will clearly see the ramifications of any changes you would like to make. We never really know the implications of our actions until they manifest. The point is to determine whether the event contributed to our spiritual evolution.

How did my deeds affect others?

One important piece of your life review is to determine how your thoughts and actions affected others. Every move we make affects those around us. Your actions certainly make an impression on your greater environment through the ripple effect. However, you should be most concerned about the people who are now or have ever been in your immediate circle of influence. In the myriad of events that come to mind through the process of discovery, how did your words and actions change the lives of others? If you are compelled to make comparisons, how do you support your conclusions? What specific changes are you aware of that took place in their lives? Do you feel it benefited or hurt them? If you think you would change the situation in any way, then this may indicate that your beliefs and values need to be reconsidered. This is a wonderful opportunity for you to expand in new ways. After all, we are mandated to expand our consciousness in every direction. Think growth. That is the nature of "The All" and of all things that spring from it. Embrace it.

Did I contribute to society and the lives of other people, or was I only concerned with my own self-indulgent pursuits?

One of the most highly prized attributes one can strive for is a generous spirit. Giving of one's self is a far greater thing than the desire to satisfy one's passing fancies. Showing kindness is an act of generosity. Have you been kind in your lifetime? Can you say that you had been good to your friends and relatives, even when you were reluctant? Each person should strive to rise above the madness of the world. We should work to extinguish the fires of hatred and misery. This is the direction humanity must go. We all need to contribute in the best way we know how. Even just a little effort makes a difference. These spiritual acts help us in our own mission. When you look at your life, do you see an overly selfish person or one who has done her best to encourage others? Remember Michael Jackson's "Man in the Mirror." That's the idea. We endeavor to do this on all levels. This is not an easy task. The good news is that we have an eternity to get it right. Forever may be an intimidating thought, but time is nothing we need to worry about.

Did I serve others and make others a priority in my life?

Service is the hallmark of an enlightened person. Jesus was a servant, as were Gandhi and Mother Theresa. They knew the great secret – " It's not about me. It's about others." This can be a hard lesson to learn. It's even harder to put into practice. It may take many lifetimes to accept this tenet. We are given over to pleasure, and it is difficult to break away from this lifestyle. I'm not saying that you can't live comfortably in your pursuit of perfection, but hedonism does not imply a great desire to work on the bigger picture.

It is not necessary for you to sacrifice your well-being or your prized possessions to be of service to others. However, that is your choice. Some people choose to follow that path. Service comes in time, money, and in other forms. Think about what it means to be a servant. Picture it in your mind's eye. Give it consideration. Does this image fit with what you have done up until now? Have you done your part? Maybe you played the role of a parent, soldier, employee, or teacher, for example. Can you think of specific examples that illustrate how you have added successful experiences to this part of your evolution? Do you feel that you were lacking in this area? What can you do to make a difference now, or in your next life, if you are leaning in that direction?

Did I live in harmony with the universe? Or did I cause an imbalance?

Did you operate against natural, moral, ethical, and decent laws? Again, did your thoughts and actions contribute to the harmony of the Universal Consciousness? Did you promote a peaceful co-existence among all people with whom you had relationships? This is not as mystical as it may sound. It just means that you maintained positive relationships within the networks that you created. Did people speak well of you in your earlier years? If you were bad-mouthed by your peers, then ask yourself why. Is it because you were an unsettling energy in the circles you frequented? Do specific incidents come to mind? Can you break these incidents down to determine which of your beliefs created the negative attitudes and which led to the disruptive events? This is heavy-duty work, but it will benefit you in what will become your future.

Were all of my relationships complete? If not, is this something I need to work on in a subsequent incarnation?

Do you have any loose ends to tie up in your relationships? Take notice of what I am about to say. Do not allow important relationships to fall by the wayside because of an overbearing ego. By the way, all of your relationships are important, even the one that you have with your mail carrier. You should do your best to maintain positive relations with everyone you meet. Even if they do not reciprocate, at least you can feel good knowing you made an honest effort. If there are things you wish you had done ten years ago, do them now. If there is something you have always wanted to say to someone, say it, just so long as you don't create complications. If you have something to confess, maybe you should consider it. Use your common sense in doing this. Don't get yourself into hot water over something that is completely inconsequential. You want to lose your regret, grudges, and bitterness before moving on. These emotions hold you back. You don't need to be hanging around the earthly plane wishing you had done one thing or another before making your transition. I know you will have other matters to take care of in the afterlife.

After contemplating these questions, can you say with confidence that you have met all of your tests and challenges according to your own measure of success? If you believe that this is not the case, and you are nearing your transition, is it possible that you will want to return to this world for another go at it? What kind of plan will you put together? What will it look like? What will you do differently?

After a careful life examination using your inner resources, you should be nicely positioned to give yourself a grade for your overall performance. If you are far from your transition, give yourself a grade on what you have done to this point. This grade is useful only as a measure for identifying overall strengths and weaknesses. It is not to be used as a rating of pass or fail.

Having gone through all of these questions and reviewing your experiences, you should now be able to tie them together like a jigsaw puzzle. All events are part of a general pattern. Like a river, your experiences split at certain points and go their own way. This is because of the various obstacles and challenges that bend the river, much like large rocks. These detours form new patterns. They all come from the

Source and return to it. When you have discovered the patterns of your life, you will see that they reveal much about yourself. They tell you how you lived your life. Does your life show a pattern of success? If the answer is no, are there pieces of the puzzle missing? Do all of the pieces go together? This is just a metaphor of course, but it serves to illustrate how you should be able to make an accurate statement about the completion or collapse of your missions.

If you are at the end of your life and you have determined that it would be best for you to continue your trek toward perfection in this world, you should realize that you will have further guidance and training on the other side. Self-examination is a lifelong process that carries over into the next world. Your self-examination on this side only aids you in further reflection on your life on the other side. In this life, you might start thinking about how your next life will look. How will it be different from the last? What will you work on? Don't be concerned with the specifics such as who your parents will be, gender, location, health, career, etc. All of these details come together when you have finished the study of your life. Also, as I said before, make sure you don't get so caught up in your self-examination that you forget to live your present life. Humans have a tendency to become absorbed in their work.

Good and Evil

When I speak of God, I like to promote the "we are one" philosophy of pantheism. If you can imagine that God is in all things, and we are in God, you will get this theory. In other words, God is not only in the picture, God IS the picture. Spiritualists give God many titles. Some of these names include Universal Mind, Universal Intelligence, Infinite Source, Cosmic Mind, Divine Intelligence, etc. I will use these names throughout this book. There is also a philosophy called *monism*, which advances the idea that all things in the universe exist as one substance. New Agers, psychics, magicians, etc. (I am not fond of these titles) commonly refer to this undefined substance as astral energy, universal energy, vital energy, life force, chi, ki, Prana, and so on. This "energy" that permeates the universe is the Cosmic Mind. The vital life force is the substance used in energy healing therapies in such common modalities as Reiki and acupuncture. It can also be used for displaying power, as we see in the martial arts. So what does this mean? It means that we are part of the source of all creation. We are part of it, and all parts are equal. Does this mean we are God? I will let you decide that. I will give you this bit of wisdom from the Bible: "God made man in his own image."

Ancient teachings instruct seekers that we do not know God (or the Source), and God does not know us. Let me shed some light on this statement. To us, God is truly mysterious and even unknowable. My impression is that we are in the process of discovering the nature of God day by day. God is also learning the ways of humans. Contact with physical reality is a unique experience for those beings that are unfamiliar with it. God is experiencing the world through us. Thus God, in its parts and as a whole, learns what it is like to be human with all the tests and challenges that come with it. Knowing that God seeks to

expand itself (as much as people, businesses, and govern-
ments do in the physical world), we do this willingly and
in most cases with enthusiasm. We hope that one day God
and man will unite as one in this particular experimental
reality we have created.

Today I was sitting in a diner with a friend. I over-
heard a rather loud customer talking to his friend about a
serious car accident he had been in some time ago. He described how his family mistakenly thought that he had
died. The man went on to say that first he went to hell and
then he went to heaven. He stated that when he met God,
God told him jokes. He then laughed and explained to his
companion that he (the man) is a joker, so God is also a
joker. Clearly, this little story illustrates how we create our
own heaven and hell. The man in this story created the god
of his imagination.

All of us expend at least a little mental sweat thinking
about where we are going to spend eternity. Most of us
have some thoughts on how this will go down. In most
cases, our fundamental beliefs come from our parents or
guardians. Your parents' beliefs were installed by their
parents. This chain continues uninterrupted through many
generations. The belief system of a person's larger community also plays a vital role. Nearly all major religions
have taken hold this way. In most cases, we are offered no
alternatives to choose from in how we think about death. It
takes a strong will to break away from the crowd.

As in life, in the afterlife you can have whatever God
you desire. If you want to worship a fearsome Viking god,
you got it. If you want to interact with a beautiful Greek
goddess, consider it done. If you believe an all-powerful
and all-knowing entity named Donald Duck can fulfill
your spiritual needs, then you are certainly an uncommon
thinker. In any case, it's allowed. The universal mind has

placed no restrictions on your creative abilities when it comes to death. You can have any kind of afterlife experience you desire. This is something you may want to consider.

The fact that our perception of death is influenced by our parents, caretakers, teachers, religious leaders, the media, and many other informational sources can make for a scary situation. By this, I mean that we adopt preconceived notions of where we will go when we die, if anywhere. As I discussed, these beliefs will manifest and become reality. I promise you, if your pastor told you that upon death, the Holy Spirit will transport you to the pearly gates with Saint Peter standing by with the Book of Life in his hands, this is the first thing you will see.

Hell

It is just as certain that you will experience a biblical hell if a priest has convinced you that is where you are going. A book came out a couple of years ago in which the author, a devout Christian, apparently projected out of his body and landed straight smack dab in the middle of the infernal kingdom. During this fateful trip, the author witnessed hideous demons, fire, brimstone, people burning, etc. I am sure that this author will defend the validity of his experience to the very end. And he is right. He had a *bona fide* moment in hell. This was his personal hell that he mentally created. It is as real as anything in this life. Yet, it was illusory, just as this world is. Remember "Merrily, merrily, merrily. Life is but a dream"? That's true. Well, sort of.

This can best be explained by referring back to the law of attraction. Just as this law has a hand in what we experience in this reality, it functions with equal force on the other side, except that in the etheric realms, we see our thoughts manifest instantly. If you were to think of a house, then the house would appear without any delay, exactly as you imagined it. It will be as solid as the house you may now occupy. In the case of hell, this can be quite unfortunate.

There are numerous religious sects that preach about original sin and the corruption of the soul as a means of keeping their church members subservient. Those followers, who suffer with intense and unremitting feelings of guilt at their time of death, inevitably face that which has been implanted into their subconscious by their supposed defenders. We have to keep in mind that the person who is in this situation is responsible for this. Yes, it's true that the person had a helping hand from his friends in creating this horrible prison, but ultimately the guilt-ridden person did it to himself. We can blame no one but ourselves for situations that we create, here or there.

Note that the closer you are to God, the closer you will also be to the devil. What this means is that if you follow any faith that supports the existence of good and evil, you are that much more at risk of encountering a wicked deity upon death. Therefore, your belief in a conventional God has predisposed you to a fate you would probably rather avoid. This is a strange twist. Do not take it that I am against all organized religions. Many of the popular religions have wonderful teachings. Still, I do not agree with some of their oppressive doctrines.

In the multiverse, which we generally refer to as the afterlife, you will find that there are entities we manufacture with our powerful imagination which manifest into reality, and there are entities which exist of their own accord. This is also true of our dream characters. The devil and other evil creatures are manifestations of our negative thinking. I'm sure everyone can appreciate that statement. Your negative thoughts and emotions such as fear, resentment, bitterness, worthlessness, and powerlessness will trigger the creative forces of the Universal Consciousness to produce the nonphysical and sometimes physical embodiment of evil. I have personally witnessed this.

One night at about midnight, I sat up in bed and observed my body still sleeping. The room was pitch black when I went to bed. However, at this time the darkness had a luminous quality to it, so that I could see well. It was like having night vision. I briefly looked around the room and saw nothing. As I looked up, I observed a dark cloud slowly swirling near the ceiling. I could see the fine details of the cloud. It was like black smoke. I realized that this was a conscious entity. I could sense an unmistakable evil emanating from it. Feeling the presence of evil is indeed a rare experience. It's extremely hard to describe. Then again, I don't want to. After understanding what I was dealing with, I fell back to sleep, and that called an end to my out-of-body experience. Some of you may have experienced the dark cloud. I have heard similar stories mentioned in other books, on internet forums, and from friends. I am sure that some people would dismiss this event as a nightmare. That is expected.

This example offers believers a good example of how a negative attitude will produce undesired results. As I have been preaching throughout this section, you can actually manifest these thoughts into reality as *bona fide* evil beings. I can admit that this dark cloud could have been a manifestation independent of my own thoughts. It may have come from another realm to feed on my energy. The dark cloud would then be designated an astral parasite. Either way the principle of attraction still applies here. Your thoughts will create or attract these entities. They can be harmful to you and to the well-being of your psychic body. Of course, such things cannot extinguish your light, but they can certainly make you sick. Practice controlling your thoughts to prevent this from happening. Read something uplifting. Watch comedies on television. Attend exciting social events. It's fine for you to continue reading this book.

I will also mention that there exist places in the multiverse that are undesirable planes to visit. Lingering in these spheres can be unpleasant. In these realms, there are creatures some would consider evil. They are nasty entities that feed on negative emotions. The entity we call the "grim reaper" would be one of these. Many people have seen this creature. I do not think the grim reaper performs the job that is attributed to him. That tale belongs to folklore.

There are magical groups that seek to access these rather unpleasant beings, thinking they have special powers. These entities are sure to go along with their beliefs. You may know people in this world who act tough to make you believe in their superiority. The truth is that we have far more power than these negative energy beings do, which is why conjurers are able to call upon them and command them. However, dark spirits usually have a hidden agenda and are not to be trusted. Personally, I am not impressed by their pretense. I suggest avoiding these creatures if possible. They are of no consequence to our mission. If they should show up, just ignore them. If you give them any attention or show fear, they will be obliged to hang around.

Perfection

Perfection is a misunderstood concept. I want to bring some clarity to it. Perfection is not about reaching a perfect state. You are never going to be able to say that your house is perfect. Even when it was brand spanking new, it was not perfect. Our interpretation of an object or situation does not represent its ideal state. We all have opinions about how good something is. The object or situation is independent of our judgments. Therefore, perfection is just a label.

On the other hand, an object or situation is perfect on its own. It is "perfect in the moment." This statement can be difficult to buy if the parking enforcement officer has your car towed. You probably won't be saying the situation is perfect. This is because you do not have a clear understanding of perfection. We are talking about higher knowledge. These ideas are hard to apprehend with a worldly mind.

Although an object or situation is perfect in the moment, an illumined mind will also view perfection as a steady upward climb. It is important to understand that humans are perpetually evolving into higher beings through the stages of life and death. We do not find perfection even at the end of our reincarnational cycle. We will move on to new challenges in higher spheres of consciousness. That is the nature of the universe; all things evolve. There are no exceptions to this rule.

Some religions even choose to make their god perfect. They have determined that God should know that which has yet to be made known. Let me tell you that God only knows as much as we know about the human experience. Beyond that, it strives to expand its awareness by seeking perfection. This is the meaning of perfection. There is perfection in the moment and perfection in the change. Perfection moves forward in an unbroken chain. At each illusory step in the overall progression of an entity's evolution, there is perfection. This is not a contradiction in terms, if you think about it. This idea may seem a little abstract at first, but if you apply some meditative contemplation, you will understand.

This is markedly different from the perfection we know: in that, the perfection we seek is unattainable. We have to be cautious, because the human version of perfection can be harmful to our psyche. People develop severe psychiatric disorders because of their inability to achieve their ideals. It can be incredibly frustrating when we attempt to reach an unreasonable and improbable goal.

There is nothing wrong with falling short of your expectations, as long you get back in the saddle and try again. This is the process of perfection. It requires patience and determination. It sounds insane to have a never-say-die mentality when we are working towards an ideal that can never be achieved. Repetition becomes madness. Realize that you are improving at each illusory step. By putting a ceiling on our projects, such as writing a book, we can come to a place where we conclude that it is perfect. There is a term called "good enough." This phrase has a bad rap in our society. Good enough means we can have our sanity. It does not put an end to evolution. Neither does it imply settling for less. It merely states that we have gone as far as we can, and must now go in another direction. This action will help us to gain a different perspective. A person who continually picks at an object or situation needlessly does not improve it. If it were a painting, it would be better to start over with a new canvas. This is what "finished" looks like. That is perfection. It is not creating an inferior work. Good enough is a subjective term. It is only possible for the creator or person in charge to decide when the situation qualifies for the "finished" label. This is why we must have a healthy attitude towards our creations. There comes a time when we must allow our creations to fly free.

Perfectionists often feel that they have fallen short of the expectations of others when they are criticized. Even constructive criticism feels like a failure. If you are some-one who feels that you do your very best, but are unable to accept constructive criticism, you may be a perfectionist. Let's call this condition "the perfectionist complex." I'm giving it this name whether or not this term is being used for some other purpose. Perfectionists feel that mistakes are unacceptable. If you tell a master chef or an artist that their work could be better, they are likely to explode at you. This person may even cry. Perfectionists take things personally. They internalize harmless criticisms and turn them into assaults on their character.

Perfectionists are the biggest critics. Many of them are great at identifying other people's apparent flaws. On the other hand, perfectionists choose to tear apart their own work looking for some minor blemish. They split hairs trying to reach a dubious state of excellence. Don't get me wrong. We are supposed to do our best to improve our po-sition with every step we take. It's okay to reach for the stars; just don't drive yourself crazy with the minute de-tails. Learn to say, "Good enough, I am happy with the results."

True perfection, whether it is the perfection of con-sciousness or perfection of earthly pursuits, is one that in-volves high ideals. Our perception of perfection is valid for each one of us. Pursuit of perfection is the absolute truth. Our human nature leaves us no choice but to pursue this high ideal. This is passion. Following our passion is our only option. Otherwise, we cannot grow as spiritual be-ings. Societies that follow conventional standards live in confusion and misery. Perfection encourages us to live up to our potential. Again, those of us who choose to work toward perfection in an unhealthy fashion will experience it that way. It's a graceful balancing act on a slippery surface. I believe it is called ice-skating.

This is not a philosophical discourse. I find philosophy tends to be a bit on the intellectual side. A friend once said to me that philosophers do a lot of talking but get nothing done. I am repeating this statement in my words just for clarification. At times, I do find light philosophy useful in discussing metaphysical concepts. If you enjoy philosophy, by all means continue to enjoy it. The world needs passionate individuals in this area.

The True Meaning of Life

We should ask ourselves "What is the point of all this?" Why does the Divine Source seek to do this, besides fulfilling its mission to expand? I'm sure the information being received is for more than nourishment. Many religions believe that God knows all. In truth, God only knows everything it knows at the present moment. God continually seeks to perfect itself. Maybe the Divine Source is maturing. There is always room for improvement. From the moment we are born, we experience life in every wonderful moment. We collect information right up to the time of our departure from this plane, with the hope that we will have gained a degree of wisdom.

It's clear to me that our earthly lives are meant for a higher purpose. We are here for a reason. If physical reality didn't matter, then we wouldn't be here. We need to stay focused on our mission(s) and deal with whatever comes our way. Knowing the truth, we can allow ourselves to step back and keep from being absorbed into the chaos of the world. We also want to enjoy the good things in life without over-indulging.

The opposing realities we perceive as the material world and the spiritual world come from our inability to perceive the other side. I came to this conclusion after receiving illumination from the higher intelligences. Any metaphysicist understands that everything we know about our reality is based on the stimuli we receive through our five recognized senses. All of the amazing sensations we enjoy are experienced as taste, touch, smell, sight, and sound. This includes such things as a breathtaking landscape, beautiful music, tasty food, the touch of a loved one, and the smell of spring. I believe that these rich sensations are incentives for us to come here and experience this reality. The magnificent colors and vibrant sounds fill our senses. Why wouldn't any bored entity want to come here for some fun? It also helps that we are given incentives like food, sex, and other pleasurable stimulation; otherwise, we would not be motivated to eat and procreate. Humans need to be motivated to get things done. We can be lazy at times.

The Universal Mind has chosen to create the elaborate illusion that we call physical reality to carry out the Great Work. Although it is very accurate to call the material world an illusion, it is also misleading. I want to assure you that the physical reality does exist. Just In case you were worried. There are certain groups that believe the material universe is of no consequence. They believe that matter doesn't matter. These questionable schools of thought teach their students that only spiritual paths are worth pursuing. Because of this, these dedicated practitioners spend their precious time with their heads in the clouds. These misinformed souls are unable to appreciate and acknowledge the material existence. I call recognition of the physical truth "corporeal acceptance." Those individuals who refuse corporeal acceptance ignore the common reality in favor of the unknown. Their beliefs may prevent them from tackling difficult situations. Those who reject the physical truth can be useless in emergencies. Fear can paralyze these people to the extent that they choose to deny the existence of a crisis. How can a person be effective when he denies the world? It's far better to face the truth than to distract your mind with thoughts of heaven. We do, in fact, live in a material world and we must behave according to this certainty. I am not trying to contradict myself. It's important to strike a balance between our pursuit of higher worlds and our mission(s) in this world.

Let's also recognize that the ego plays an important role in the human odyssey. Many people and groups advocate pushing the ego out. The ego is necessary for us to navigate through physical reality. We would be lost without it. There is a difference between subduing the ego and doing away with it. We need to keep the ego from getting out of control. The ego is the part of us that must be tamed so that we do not lose ourselves to the material world. We do not want to develop an inflated ego. If you need help and are a man, imagine losing your libido. This thought will deflate your ego. If you are a woman, imagine gaining 20 pounds. I realize this may sound sexist, but it illustrates my point.

My goal here is that we recognize the truth that the material world exists, as does the spiritual. Does that make sense? We must be aware of both worlds. There should be a balance between the internal and external environments.

On Certain Entities

Little People

You also see the "little people" when you are in your light body (astral). In this supernatural category, we have leprechauns, fairies, elves, and more. I realize this idea may sound preposterous to some of you, but there are reasons why these creatures have been so popular throughout history. There is nothing original about this idea. Hundreds of people have encountered them over the centuries. Anyone who has done any serious research on mythical creatures will come to the same conclusion. They are not physical in our terms, which is why we do not see these diminutive "servants," if you will, walking around. Okay, so I'm talking about invisible elves and leprechauns.

I would like to refer you to a book I read when I was a teenager. Look at *Field Guide to the Little People*, by Nancy Arrowsmith (Llewellyn, 1977). It will help you to become familiar with the many Earth spirits who work alongside us. This book doesn't go into the metaphysical aspects surrounding these subhuman beings. However, it provides a good account of their nature and general disposition. You can never make sweeping judgments when referring to any particular group, but there are usually propensities common to each kind of little people.

The little people are the ones who tend to the maintenance of this planet. Most of us never think about how the work gets done. Please allow me to digress for a moment on that point. There's a reason why everything works so perfectly in the universe. We get just what we need to stay alive and flourish as a higher species. If there isn't an omnipotent being orchestrating the dance of the universe, then surely there are large numbers of entities who are responsible for this big job. You can thank the little people and elementals. Some say little people are paying their dues, in order to become human. You could compare this notion to that of an angel paying her dues in order to earn her wings. This idea was popularized in "It's a Wonderful Life" starring James Stewart. These little tales are probably false, but they make good stories for children.

Angels

Contrary to popular ideas put forth by organized religions, angels are not soldiers enforcing God's laws. While it's true angels are the agents of the Universal Consciousness, they beings who do their work for the good of humanity. Angels do not appear haphazardly. They always come with a divine purpose.

Angels intervene to facilitate change. There may be a great change about to take place in the world. We may wonder why angels do not intervene to prevent tragedies such as the 2004 Indian Ocean Tsunami, as well as the many other awful occurrences throughout history. The reason is this: angels intervene on behalf of the civilization; they serve to further its spiritual growth. It's possible that preventing a national disaster will hinder our mass evolution. Such events serve to teach us valuable lessons and help us grow spiritually. Preventing these tragic events would only set us back. You see, the pain we experience in our lifetime serves a divine purpose. The Collective Consciousness allows terrible things to happen in order to carry out the Master Plan. Angels are obliged to observe the will of the Divine. It's not that we have a cruel and uncaring God. God is love. It's all about our spiritual growth.

This principle also works on a personal level. Perhaps there is a certain lesson we must learn from the death of a loved one. These lessons may need to be learned at the expense of our happiness. This explanation is not meant to help you feel better about your loss, but at least it will help you understand the process. The good things we receive usually have nothing to do with why we think we want them. The same is true if we lose them. If we always got what we wanted, there would be little progress in our evolution. Then you could say there would be little point in pursuing this adventure. Again, angels work for our best interests. This mandate does not always coincide with what makes us happy. We get a bit confused in this area.

Aliens

First, let me start by saying that alien life forms only exist extra-dimensionally. They are not on other planets. My understanding on this matter is that there is no life in outer space. I know this through my own intuitive moments with the Universal Consciousness. I know that some people will fiercely argue this point. This is just my personal theory. Please feel welcome to keep your own beliefs.

Alien beings exist in multitudes throughout the multiverse. They may or may not know we exist. The more metaphysically and spiritually advanced creatures are familiar with our history, although few of them have an interest in what goes on here. These civilizations do not know any more about us than we know of them. They have no reason to be involved in our development. Why would any advanced people want to invade and conquer our planet? These extra-dimensional alien races have everything they need to live a satisfying existence. They want for nothing. In that same breath, I will admit the possibility that hostile alien races exist somewhere in the multiverse.

Legendary places such as Shambala and Irem, "the nameless city," are among the many domains of the multiverse. That is only the beginning. Alien life forms of all kinds inhabit the infinite multiverse. They all have different levels of intelligence and technology. They come in all shapes and sizes. Some look like the classic Greys that we see in motion pictures.

The Greys have been described by witnesses as gray-skinned aliens, short in stature and lacking human features such as noses and ears. These descriptions vary greatly with the observer. The first recognized encounter with the Greys is said to be the Hill abduction. Betty and Barney Hill claim they were abducted by aliens while driving in New Hampshire on September 19, 1961. The story of the Hills has been reproduced in the 1966 book *Interrupted Journey*, and in the 1975 movie *The UFO Incident*. The Greys have been the subject of countless novels, magazine articles, and movies over the past decades. Some groups have gone as far as to implicate these mysterious beings in their new world order conspiracies. Most reports of the Greys are inaccurate. Some of these sightings are outright hoaxes.[1]

The *Greys* are often encountered during hallucinogenic excursions. People also see the Greys during out-of-body experiences. I feel strongly that OOBEs give a fairly accurate picture of how the Greys appear. The Greys occasionally enter our reality using physical bodies and vehicles. They are obviously an advanced race and well-versed in metaphysics. They seek enlightenment for our world. The Greys work behind the scenes (like many other non-human entities) to provide various kinds of support for our spiritual growth. The Greys respect our perception of a

---

[1] About.com, *1961-The Hills: Abducted by Aliens,* http://www.about.com, accessed June 6, 2012.

seemingly secluded universe. This is why there is little known about the Greys. Their appearance in the world seems to us to occur at random times. They reveal themselves only when it serves the purposes of the master plan.

The *Pleiadeans*, also known as Nordic Aliens or Aryan Aliens, have been the subject of much discussion for at least several decades. Reporters describe Pleiadeans as six to seven feet tall with long blond hair and blue eyes. In most cases, the male of the species is encountered. Claims of visits by the aliens were common during the 1950s and continued in subsequent decades.

The Pleiadeans have had a big impact on Earth's history. There have been many stories created about their culture. There may be some grain of truth to them, as there is to most stories. I am not terribly familiar with the Pleiadeans myself. However, I am certain that the Pleiadeans also exist in another etheric domain. I am confident that the Pleiadeans are a highly advanced society, especially in the mental physics department. If the Pleiadeans were once on this plane in physical form, they may still have a great interest in our activities. I'm sure one could establish a telepathic connection with them. I have heard of people who have done this.

Guides

There are people who want to help you get to where you need to be. A large number of "new age" books refer to them as guides. In some traditions, guides are referred to as "conductors." For example, the Christ is a conductor of souls. Guides rescue people from their afterlife predicaments. Guides locate these lost souls and gently rouse them out of their slumber, in order to get them back on track. Souls may have become stuck, because they do not realize they have transitioned, or due to their inability to accept the reality of their own death. This could be a person temporarily inhabiting heaven or hell (it doesn't matter what the person's religion happens to be). There are times when a person will haunt their home of fifty years, because he or she doesn't realize a transition has occurred. It could also be that a person has a strong attachment to physical life. He may be unwilling to give up his possessions or relationships. There are many reasons why people cannot move on from their earthly existence. The problem with this is that these unfortunate entities get sidetracked from their mission. Their reincarnational cycle is interrupted. After our transition, we should move on to reviewing our lives and participating in life skills training.

Guides or conductors, depending on which term you prefer, are just regular people like you and me. Living guides often do the same job as their invisible counterparts. You may even have a relationship with an incarnated guide. Also, be advised that not every psychic, new ager, guru, or person with self-awareness is a guide. Those assigned as living guides may or may not be aware of their purpose. They rescue wayward souls in their dreams, during meditation sessions, or in out-of-body journeys. Guides have no special abilities or status. Guides have simply had extensive training to do their jobs. In some ways, guides are like social workers. Guides may have other responsibilities, such as moving living persons in the right direction. Guides are charged with helping people fulfill their mission in this life. Again, a guide can do this job from the other side, or in the flesh. A living guide may have no knowledge that they are being of service to the other person. You may have run into a guide. A person who has made a big impact on your life, or helped in some way, *may* be a guide. This person who played a pivotal role in changing your life may be a full-fledged humanitarian, or perhaps it was just a chance encounter with a stranger.

Let's look at this hypothetical situation. Early in your life, you were a heavy drinker. One night you drive home from a bar completely intoxicated and crash into a guardrail on a lonely stretch of highway. When your car is engulfed in flames, an unknown Good Samaritan stops and pulls you from the wreck. He then calls 911 and disappears. If the stranger hadn't intervened, your life would have come to a painful end. As a result, you resolve to quit drinking that day. Your new lease on life opened up a world of opportunities for you. Perhaps being saved from the burning wreck allowed you to continue working on your closest relationships. Learning to maintain healthy relationships can be a person's plan for this world. The possibilities are endless.

This scenario could certainly happen. In fact, it happens all of the time. Not all of us will be guides, of course. However, we can still be of service to others. We never know what our thought-ripples will accomplish, especially if we are working with higher forces. You will usually know when a guide has entered your life. You will get that "funny feeling." Even just a slight inclination towards the spiritual side will help identify it. That feeling you get is unmistakable. You will find yourself irresistibly drawn to that person's magnetic quality. Guides usually possess a humble character and a high degree of integrity. They always seem to do the right thing. Keep your eyes peeled for them.

The White Lodge and the White Brotherhood

Many quasi-religious groups and fraternal organizations claim the White Lodge and the White Brotherhood. I draw my knowledge of the White Lodge from Rosicrucian teachings, although the White Brotherhood is not exclusive to this fellowship. My understanding of the White Lodge is far different from Rosicrucian philosophy.

The White Brotherhood exists as an organized network of illumined souls, both in this life and the next, who work to improve the human condition. For this reason, I am comfortable in stating that the White Brotherhood is simply another name for the misunderstood Illuminati. Some people will balk at my association of the two terms. That is to be expected. The Illuminati have created more controversy and conspiracy theories than any other group in recent history. While the workings of the Illuminati are shrouded in mystery for good reason, it's important that the world should know that their intentions are pure.

The name Illuminati historically refers to the Bavarian Illuminati formed by Adam Weishaupt in 1776. The order was originally given the named the "Perfectibilists." One definition for Perfectibilist comes from Wordnik (www.wordnik.com): "One who believes in the perfectibility of human nature in this life." In my mind, perfectibility is a philosophy concerned with perfection of the soul and spiritual evolution. My partiality to this definition is evident throughout this book.

Living members of the White Brotherhood or Illuminati, along with its spirit members, seek to advance the spiritual development of our race. This includes improving the condition of our global community. This is accomplished in many ways, including initiating new members into the brotherhood to increase their reach and effectiveness. The activities of the illumined ones are made secret so that they may carry out their duties undisturbed. The Illuminati spend a portion of their free time meditating and contemplating metaphysical and spiritual matters. They receive assistance from members that have departed this world, and have a continued commitment to the spiritual growth of our people.

I can assure you that the Illuminati have nothing to hide. Illuminati philosophy dictates that its members should seek out leadership positions to assist others in reaching their true potential. Everyone is capable of leadership on some level. An enlightened leader would know that he or she is not in charge, but acts as a teacher. The Illuminati is not an elite society of capitalists bent on world domination and the creation of a new world order. It has no special knowledge that cannot be rightfully claimed by any prospective member willing to work for it. The White Brotherhood is not hidden to the point that it cannot be found with a little effort.

Drugs and Mental Illness

Psychedelics

The body has been designed to block out all external stimuli that doesn't conform to the common reality. Psychoactive substances fill neuron synapses allowing a "Psychonaut" to encounter a small portion of the other side for a short time. This is a much-skewed view of the other side and can provide very little insight as to what the explorer is witnessing. A "trip" is not the same as an authentic out-of-body experience, as far as sensory feedback is concerned. A genuine out-of-body experience allows one to get his or her bearings and, after repeated projections, to make sense of things. Psychedelics, when used recreationally, permit imagery and sensations that are all but meaningless. Most people use psychedelics as party drugs and have no knowledge of what they are dealing with. The afterlife is not a game. The imagery perceived can be frightening and leave the unsuspecting user with any number of mental impairments. Some powerful hallucinogens such as Ayahuasca, a mixture of plants used for divinatory purposes by indigenous people, have been perverted by industrialized countries for entertainment.

While "tripping," you may experience something similar to the visuals in the Beatles' "Lucy in the Sky with Diamonds," but you are not getting the whole picture. You only see shades of the truth. Therefore, you are getting nothing profoundly meaningful from these trips, even though the information may seem deep at the time. Getting bits and pieces of something as massive as the multiverse through a series of acid trips is nothing but a waste of time. I have never personally used psychedelics. I know enough about them to steer clear of them.

My belief is that our bodies prevent us from perceiving the invisible universe. We are designed to focus our senses on physical reality, which may be why we have only five primary senses to work with. Our extra sensory perception requires development in order to make use of it. It's possible that someday scientists will discover the biological mechanisms that keep us from seeing the etheric realms. Perhaps a lack of certain chemicals prevents us from receiving the mental images that characterize the nature of the multiverse. As I suggested earlier, chemicals like LSD and DMT allow us to view portions of the multiverse, but without clarity. I have no chemistry background, so this is just speculation on my part. I do have an innate sense, which counts for more than our current state of scientific knowledge in this unexplored area.

Mental Illness

Psychiatric illnesses such as schizophrenia provide the afflicted person with a particularly disturbing way to experience the multiverse. In my earlier years, I held a couple of positions in the mental health sector working with patients on employment and housing matters. This was quite challenging, as one has to relate to people who are operating under a different paradigm. Those with conditions like schizophrenia and bipolar disorder speak of things that people in the common reality cannot understand. These exceptional people are describing things that demonstrate the truth. However, their conversations have no real relevance to our experience.

Just so there are no misconceptions, I have never experienced anything similar to a psychotic episode characteristic of schizophrenia. I am talking about "hallucinations." My knowledge of this condition is second hand, yet I have gained a sufficient understanding of the physical and nonphysical mechanisms behind it.

I realize that psychotic episodes can be frighteningly real. I would compare them to a vivid nightmare. The imagery is often the same, but the level of awareness is different, since this kind of experience should not take place in the waking state. What is the nature of these powerful visual images? First, I do not think they are hallucinations. These disturbing images have their origin in the same areaas our creative imagination, just as medical doctors would tell us. However, these creatures are fully aware of themselves and have their own vital essence. It's just a matter of determining how real they are by our standards. I realize that this can be a scary statement for the psychiatrist.

Our body chemistry has allowed these entities to escape from us. Just know that we have control over these mental states. We retain the ability to tame the sensory manifestations that spring from them.

When we encounter mentally ill persons, we find ourselves uncomfortable and even frightened. We try to distance ourselves from them out of fear. This condition comes from the inability to relate. Their sometimes bizarre behavior is an obstacle to creating a personal connection. This is extremely frustrating to the mentally ill person who cannot communicate what he or she is experiencing to the rest of the world.

This misunderstanding of the mentally ill population has pushed them into the darkness, where they remain in silence. Many "higher functioning" persons have chosen to keep their illnesses to themselves in order to avoid the stigma that comes with mental illness. This is a shame, since mentally ill persons have so much to offer the world. Their unique perspective on the illusion of life is invaluable. They see things in ways that others cannot. Mentally ill persons have made great contributions in every field of human endeavor. We can look to such historical figures as Charles Dickens, Pablo Picasso, Isaac Newton, and Winston Churchill as examples of the role the mentally ill have played in the development of our kind. Their lives were gifts to us. Even now, there are those mentally ill persons who enrich our lives in countless ways.

In organizing my thoughts for this book, I gained special insight into the psychiatric condition known as Attention Deficit Disorder (ADD). The distinguishing characteristic of ADD is the inability to concentrate on one task for any length of time. Attention Deficit Hyperactivity Disorder (ADHD) also shares this rather broad definition along with its own special features. Many of you are probably familiar with these common psychiatric disorders and may even know someone diagnosed with one of them.

ADD is fascinating in that these people are involuntarily trying to access multiple levels of physical reality at one time. Those living with ADD seem to be rapidly moving from one focus to the next. There is, of course, but one reality and focus. Humans are only able to access only one slice of reality at a time. Even as humans can only have one thought at a time.

These layers of reality may be extremely close to each other and have slightly different content. The reception mechanism of a person diagnosed with ADD does not allow him or her to focus on one reality. Their attention quickly bounces back and forth in an effort to grasp all of the choices. In the common reality, humans focus on one thing at a time. That is a given.

Most humans do not experience ADD because of a biological mechanism that blocks this kind of astral vision. This mechanism is most likely a chemical process. ADD appears when the biological shield has been compromised. Many mental health conditions emerge because a safety mechanism in the body has been interrupted.

A meditation routine can help bring ADD under control. Meditation teaches a person to slow down and consider each thought before acting on it. Meditation gives a person time to sort out the various thoughts that come rushing in. It takes time to develop this ability, but it can be had by anyone with the patience to practice it.

You might be wondering about multitasking. It is a rare talent to be able to do two things at the same time, the exception being the autonomic nervous system, which is governed by our subconscious.

On the other hand, having multiple focuses is the normal operating state for human entities in the afterlife. Entities of certain domains commonly use multiple focuses to access several layers of reality at one time. On the otherside, the veils are lifted. For example, past, present, and future can be seen by human entities all at once, since time is nonexistent outside of this reality. I realize this can be incredibly confusing. Remember, the other side does not correspond to our physical laws. Time is very illusory.

It's possible that many of the smaller creatures sharing our world can focus on more than one layer of reality. This ability is most evident in insects. Since we cannot identify this suppressed ability in ourselves, it's difficult to see it elsewhere.

Those individuals labeled with ADD are capable of maintaining multiple focuses. This can be a problem in the common reality. We aren't meant to operate that way. Those labeled with ADD must struggle to maintain a sense of normalcy. It can be a tough boat to row. One has to work a little harder at trying to navigate the material world. ADD can also be a gift with the creative expression it brings to the table. It's not all doom and gloom.

We must realize that mental illness has nothing to do with the mind. The term "mental illness" is flawed. The problem is not typically mental, except in certain circumstances as with phobias. The mind is always perfect. With mental illness, there is always brain impairment. The information a person receives through his five senses cannot be interpreted correctly by the brain. Therefore, the brain sends faulty information to the mind resulting in a distorted version of the common reality.

My understanding is that illnesses such as schizophrenia and bipolar disorder have their roots in imbalances of chemicals such as dopamine, serotonin, and norepinephrine. Perhaps these imbalances have similar effects to those of psychedelics. It just shows how our bodies are complicated organic machines. It's also true that the human body is sensitive. Some otherworldly engineer did a good job with the design. The technicians that put our reality together created everything in a very precise manner. However, it seems that it doesn't take much for us to have a misfire.

Glimpses of the other side while we are living can be scary because we have no frame of reference for such things, and therefore we have no point of comparison. How do you describe a creature you have never seen before and which has absolutely no resemblance to anything that exists in our world? That's a very difficult task. We describe things based on what we already know. It's almost impossible to do with our limited vocabulary.

Dimensions of Reality

Time and Space

There is an agreement between Cosmic Administrators and humanity that time and space exist in this reality. It has to, in order for our society to work as it should. Can you imagine saying to your boss, "Time doesn't exist so I'll be at work as soon as I get there"? I'm sure that wouldn't fly. Time has its place in the universe. We see time as a series of moments strung together. These moments present themselves in the context of yesterday, today, and tomorrow. You could also see this as past, present, and future. The truth of the matter is that the past no longer exists in our reality, and the future is an infinite number of probabilities. Time is nothing more than a single moment stretched into infinity. Therefore, the past, present, and future exist all at once. This can be confusing to the living. I can only say that this will make perfect sense when you have made your transition. Time as we know it will seem unnecessary. I suppose that is why in some religions it is called eternity. Both life and death have no beginning or end. It has been and always will be.

This simple notion that time is illusory should completely solve most of our everyday problems. You no longer have to worry about what happened in the past. You may choose to dwell on a situation from your past, but that is a completely different matter. Don't worry about what happened in the past. As for the future, you needn't worry about that either. You are creating the future as you go along. You do this moment by moment. So make your plans with the understanding that they are subject to change.

I know many of you understand the concept of timelessness. Lack of time means living in the now. I see it as a place of power and freedom. Everything happens in the present. In fact, we cannot work from any place other than the present. Just knowing this should remove any anxiety we harbor. Keep yourself focused in the moment.

Space is similar to time in that it also is an illusion. It's simple enough to state that space is an illusion, but it's difficult to explain. Let me put it this way. Humans like to compare things. We like to think that one object is bigger than another. In other words, a 6'7" basketball player is taller than a four-year-old child. Yet there are things bigger than a 6'7" basketball player and smaller than a four-year-old child. Does that invalidate our original judgments? How do we deal with this paradox? That's easy. Size is an essential feature of the physical reality. It is a measurement. This includes length, width, and depth. Three-dimensional reality could not exist without this perception. We are always comparing objects and situations. Remember your mother saying, "Your brother (or sister) is good at math; why can't you do it?"

The idea of space as a hallucination is a little hard to swallow. If I said to you, "The traveling distance between Boston and New York City is imagined," you would laugh. This is because you can get into your car and go there, expending several hours of driving time and hundreds of miles in the process. This is hard evidence. My response to this is, "Wherever you go, there you are." Let's put it this way. When you stand in one part of a room, you say, "I am here." Now when you move to another part of the room, you can still say, "I am here" with confidence. Just as you are always in the "now," you are always "here." In the afterlife, you don't travel from point A to point B. That is not necessary. As beings of pure consciousness, we are able to think of where we want to be and poof, we are there, just like that. We may experience the sensation of traveling within and between some realms in our light body, but the phenomenon of distance is all but an illusion. That's also the case in this life, although we do not see it.

Close your eyes for a moment and imagine a landmark in New York City. Maybe you would like to visualize the Statue of Liberty. Once you can clearly see it, shift your focus and imagine Washington D.C. For simplicity, try the White House. When you see it clearly, open your eyes. You have just traveled from N.Y.C. to D.C. instantaneously. "Wait!" you say. "That is just my imagination. That's not real." Not true. Your imagination is very real. I will get into this later. Now let's try time travel. This is easy. Think of a pleasant experience you had as a child. Picture yourself there. Focus in on the colors, sounds, and the feelings you had at that time. Feel it really strongly as if you are reliving it. When you can re-experience the event as if you are there, hold the moment briefly and then let it go. You are welcome to stay with it for as long as you like, if you are enjoying the experience.

You just traveled into the past. This exercise clearly illustrates the nature of space. This mode of travel occurs in what some psychedelic drug users call "hyperspace." I consider hyperspace to be an experience one has while moving through the multiverse. Another term for this medium is the "astral space." It's a lot like the internet. You don't go to Google's homepage and then travel all the way across the World Wide Web to get to Amazon.com. That would be a ridiculous waste of time. What you would do instead is type www.amazon.com in the address bar, or you could click the website from your bookmarks. Within seconds, you are transported to Amazon's website. This is not as quick as traveling through the seamless environment of hyperspace; it does, however, make a great analogy for our purposes.

You can use this same experiment to travel into the future. You only have to visualize an event that you would like to see happen. I should hope that this would be a positive event. To do this, you would need to picture the event very clearly with all of the sights and sounds filling your senses. You should also put your emotions into it, to make it real. Use specifics, such as time and place. When you have created a complete picture in your mind, you have just created the future. That's right, a future that will surely come to pass (in some reality). As I said, we are creating the future here in the present. Some people do this intentionally and others do this by default.

Here is another experiment you can try. This works both at night and during the day. When you are walking through a large parking lot at night, look at what is in front of you a short distance ahead. You should be walking toward something, like a building. Look at the distance between you and the object. Now look down at your feet as you are walking toward the object. Look back up at the object and back down at your feet. At times, it might seem as though you are peering out of a car windshield. You can even try closing your eyes while doing this, for a slightly different experience. You will notice that you are not moving toward anything, even though you are getting closer to your destination. You will see that you are getting nowhere fast. It's as if you are walking in place.

The distance between you and the object is an illusion. This is a very difficult idea to accept. It took me many years to recognize it. No one told me about it, either. My discovery of this strange phenomenon was very much a stunning realization. It may take some time before you come to the same conclusion. Practice the exercise when you have the time.

For reference, I call the unquestioned belief in the time/space effect "temporal hypnotic amnesia." A society that accepts the time/space effect contributes to a "mass temporal hypnotic amnesia." These words do not mean that we have forgotten about the truth of time and space. In fact, it states that we are under the spell of the time/space illusion. These are concepts we consented to prior to entering into this reality. Time/space rules are necessary to operate in this plane. Space is particularly important. Think of it as a video game. The game would not work without the illusion of space.

Here is another exercise you can try in your vehicle. When you are driving on a highway, gaze into the distance and notice what is there. You may see trees or buildings. Now, take in the panoramic view of the scenery before you, and then notice what's going past you through your side door window. It will be mesmerizing after a few seconds. It will also seem as if your vehicle is motionless. After looking into the distance, look down to the nose of your vehicle and notice the pavement passing underneath. Almost hypnotically, you'll get the impression that your vehicle is not moving. This phenomenon is more than just a hallucination or your mind playing tricks on you.

Again, after practicing this for some time, you might come to the realization that your car is not moving. You have to look at this in a certain way to see what I am describing here. You will see this as the trees and cars move past you. This is just scenery and it really doesn't mean anything to us, other than serving as a backdrop for our experience. However, it's certainly real. You will not go into a deep hypnotic state doing this exercise. There is really no danger in it, as it takes less time than changing the radio station. Just stay awake and keep your awareness level up.

I know this defies our common sense, but you are seeking the truth. The truth is not found in common logic. Logic is essential to functioning in this world, but relying on reason to define reality is equivalent to grasping water in your fists. There is no spiritual growth after a certain point. Higher levels are only accessible when one sees logic for what it is. Basically, we use our reasoning skills (a mental function) to help us navigate physical reality, much like the ego. It takes a shift in conventional thinking to comprehend the things I am describing. Keep an open mind and continue to practice these simple exercises. In fact, here is another practical application of what I am teaching. The exercise below has to do with viewing the universal energy.

If you would like to observe a portion of the invisible universe, try this exercise. When you are in a relatively dark room, perhaps before you go to sleep, bring your attention to the space in the room. Gaze at the emptiness all around you. Don't fix your eyes on any particular point in the room. Just look with a sort of broken gaze into the darkness. Continue to look into the emptiness for as many days and weeks as it takes you to notice things that look like patterns of light.

I perceive things I can only describe as atoms. They completely fill my bedroom. You cannot identify one from the others. They often form patterns that I really can't make out. They seem to be white and sometimes reddish. If I close my eyes, the atoms are still there. That's because this is an internal process. I sometimes see them during the day in certain places, but they look more like halos and white energy. There is no way for me to formulate a universal method for visualizing the energy. Each person discovers his or her own way of conducting this exercise and the results he or she obtains from it.

I feel that my visual senses are so strong that I am picking up on the universal energy. This gift has benefited me in many areas of my life. First, it makes the idea of a single universal energy real to me. You know the old saying "seeing is believing"? This is especially true for me. It creates a completely different perspective on the subject. You may believe in its existence and intellectually understand its nature in a certain light, but when you see it, your thoughts on it will change. I can only guess that it must be similar in some ways to using a scanning tunneling microscope to view atoms. When you grasp the true nature of your environment, it changes your worldview. You realize that things aren't what they appear to be. This gives you the opportunity to do some reflecting. You can now give some serious consideration to where you are in your life and where you want to be. Can you see the progression here? I'll bet you didn't think you could get that far by looking into the empty space in your bedroom at night. That just goes to show you. I suppose skeptics will have their own explanations for what I am describing, but this book isn't meant to appease them.

I find the ability to see the universal energy useful to my work as a Reiki healer. Even in daylight, I can see the energy to some extent. It usually comes out as white halos or auras around people and objects. Some people have stronger auras than others, or at least I see them more intensely. Perceiving this energy allows me to direct the energy into the patient with more confidence and precision. You see, it intensifies your resolve since you can observe it around the person being treated. This mindset is conducive to creating the desired result.

That gives you a couple of good reasons to practice the exercise I have given you. Again, it may take time to get good at it, but you only have to do it for a few minutes each night or at another time of your choosing. You could combine this application with meditation if you choose. The fruits of labor will be seen at the appointed time. This may or may not coincide with your own time schedule.

When doing this exercise myself, I often see hazy outlines of things that are difficult to describe. Frequently these outlines have the appearance of rooms that do not exist in this reality. The dimension of the physical space we are standing in does not correspond to how big the room really is in metaphysical terms. It may be much larger than the size of the physical space. My wife sometimes has dreams about these rooms. She sees them in the houses where we have previously resided. We know that dreams are real and reflect our waking life. Simple dream analysis is a reliable method for assessing theories like this one. It's very possible that these rooms are occupied by unseen beings. Although an entity may be standing a distance from you or even at the far end of the multiverse, it may occupy the same space as you. I am not talking about physical space. No method exists for measuring these dimensions, since we have no way of detecting them. A mathematically-gifted metaphysicist could explain this better than I could.

You may be familiar with *The Lion, the Witch, and the Wardrobe* by C.S. Lewis. I'm referencing this story to illustrate what I have been discussing. At the beginning of this fantastic story, the Pevensie children are seen exploring the large house owned by Professor Digory Kirke. Lucy Pevensie finds herself investigating a wardrobe wherein she stumbles upon a portal to another world called Narnia. The children become the central figures in an epic battle between a great lion named Aslan and the White Witch. With this example, I am trying to open your mind to the possibility that other dimensions exist right where we stand. I'm not suggesting that you should go into closets looking for a dimensional portal. That doesn't usually happen, but this fantasy novel does bring to our attention the idea that these places may exist.

I am covering the various aspects of time and space as they relate to both physical and non-physical reality. This subject represents ideas that are very foreign to us. I'm also attempting to cover features of an extremely broad concept. It's impossible to explain the nature of time and space in a few pages. I'm sure that you understand. I'm going to discuss the vibratory nature of the multiverse, including this domain. This is the abbreviated version.

Non-physical Environments

Each sphere is separated from the others by vibratory frequencies. This is much like radio or television stations. In truth, there are no boundary lines separating these frequencies, yet we can only experience one at a time. They appear as distinct bands so that we may perceive them. It would be too confusing if everything blended into each other. We cannot access multiple layers of reality at one time. I touched on this in the ADD section. For humans, each frequency or corresponding band of frequencies is a domain unto itself. Let's be thankful for this. Domains exist on a number of bandwidths, just as our own universe does. How many frequencies are there? As many as needed. How many websites will we be able to build before we run out of space? I don't know the answer to that question, but I am thinking it is infinite.

Etheric spheres are attached by what would be considered invisible barriers. Vibratory differences in the nature of these dimensions create illusory walls that effec-

84

tively separate one universe from another. Each adjoining domain is out of the range of perception of the local inhabitants. Other civilizations may assume they are alone, just as we believe our universe is the only one that exists. Humankind believes nothing exists beyond our universe. That does not keep us from journeying through each sphere in our eergy bodies. Travel through these spheres is seamless. You can move through hyperspace from one province to the next just as you would go from one state to the next without encountering any physical resistance.

There are many systems teeming with life. Some worlds are similar to our own, and others would be unrecognizable to us. Each civilization develops along different lines and will have dissimilar technology. Some may employ light or sound as a primary means of sustaining their existence. Imagine dimensions where nothing but light exists. This light embodies numerous consciousnesses. Their personalities and intelligence would be unlike our own. However, I'm certain there are some similarities in the numerous spheres inhabited by this class of consciousness. It's also likely that there are realms whose inhabitants exist as sound. In this case, their entire domain probably exists as sound. If they have buildings or transportation, those would be composed of sound as well. Their architecture would be unlike any structures we know. You might even find that some beings and their universe exist as mathematical equations and geometric expressions. I really can't comprehend this, but intuitively I just know it to be true. These examples illustrate a few of the kinds of entities and worlds making up the multiverse. There are an endless number of exotic worlds waiting to be discovered.

I have observed entities as luminous colored shapes. They are not glowing balls of light, but more like faintly colored energies with no stable form. I could detect consciousness in these energies that clearly distinguish them from floaters. This is something you can do if you attune yourself to their vibrations. It involves opening your mind to the possibility of their existence rather than brushing them off as daydreams or hallucinations. If you attempt to make excuses for and explain away metaphysical phenomena, the opportunity for discovering a new world is lost to you. The other side is always visible if you pay attention. It is not easy if you are hyperfocused on physical reality. You must use your imagination from time to time. It is an extremely powerful tool. When a child talks about imaginary friends, you should believe them. It may be something the child created and gave life to, or it could be an extradimensional entity with a life of its own. The mind has many facets to it. It is a powerful and creative force. Don't underestimate its capability.

Creating Life

If you were a child in the 1970s, you might be familiar with the Sesame Street character Snuffleupagus. "Snuffy" was Big Bird's imaginary friend. This Sesame Street character resembled a woolly mammoth. As with all imaginary friends, no one but Big Bird could see Snuffy. Therefore, he was invisible to all the other characters on the show. In the late 1970s, other Sesame Street characters became aware of Mr. Snuffleupagus. Although Sesame Street is a children's television program, it serves as a humorous example of the power humans have to create sentient beings through the exercise of directed or inadvertent mental transmissions.

As I stated before, we are responsible for creating our own angels, demons, and every creature we dream up. We need to be careful with how we use our mental abilities. Thought forms have their own level of consciousness and intelligence. They are a result of our creative imagination. These thought forms take on a life of their own. We consistently imbue these characters with our vital energy, bringing them to life. This is a condition I call "vital essence entity infusion." I might add that the Divine Spirit gives life to us so that we may give life to the world.

It makes sense that we take steps be able to control these entities to prevent their misbehavior. This is a sensible and responsible practice. It's not as hard as it sounds. No one can keep track of his or her thought stream for long. However, it does help to contain our negative thoughts. Once these nasty life forms are set loose, they immediately seek to cause trouble for others. Conscious control of these mental nuisances can be traced back to the works of magicians and mages who are able to "command the spirits," through dark ceremonies and rituals. This part is just my conjecture.

If we were to realize the full potential of our minds, our personal reality would change dramatically. That goes for shared reality as well. I will speak on shared reality shortly.

Most of us are not "reality artists." Humans typically act as "casual creators" not even aware of our minds' mischievous behavior. Some famous reality artists include, but are not limited to, Wayne Dyer, Anthony Robbins, Cheryl Richardson, and Joel Osteen. Attractionists like Mike Dooley, the author of *Infinite Possibilities*, who live their lives with intention, are almost always reality artists. It's safe to say that greater than 99% of the population is comprised of casual creators who contribute to the world's disorder and confusion. I count myself among that number.

We must work to change that. I hope that what I am presenting here will make a difference.

Past and Future

Humans take the belief in time so seriously that some of us literally live mentally (remember mental reality is perhaps even more real than the physical) in the past or in the future. We do this when we are preoccupied with the events of the past and obsessing about the future. Naturally, this situation delays our ascent towards a higher level of existence. The plans, tests, and challenges we put together for this life come to a halt when we put ourselves in this position. Spiritual evolution can be analogous to a free flow of energy moving us along from one lesson to the next. Certain dispositions block our forward progress. These attitudes keep us from experiencing this vital flow. I don't want to be dramatic here. I just want to relate that when we engage in nonproductive behavior such as this, we are just wasting our time. Under these circumstances, we all but abandon the mission we have taken up in this life.

Interestingly, animals live in the present while preserving important memories for when they are needed. This is especially true of dogs. Our canine friends do not hold resentment, bitterness, and unresolved anger. However, it's true that they can suffer from psychological trauma. Animals generally make their point and go on with their business. Humans cling to their emotions, giving their memories the vital energy they need to remain in the present.

Children also live in the present, at least until they reach adolescence. If they are healthy, children do not worry or plan. This is a manifestation of the modern era. Centuries ago, people lived in the present. For ancient people it was a matter of survival. In most parts of the world, people were fighting to stay alive. Trying to get the necessities was a top priority. A person of that time could not dwell on the past or the future. He or she had to deal with the matter at hand. In simple terms, survival takes precedence over your insecurities.

Now, we all know reality is fraught with pain. People seek to avoid their painful circumstances by retreating to the past or escaping into the future. Although there are other ways to deal with a negative experience, the "past retreat/future escape" is a common one. This isn't a case of "Remember when we...," it's more like "Let me tell you about my life" for the next five hours. In fact, "I think I'm going to remain on this topic permanently." Compared to some of the coping techniques that change our reality past retreatism/future escapism is one of the milder courses to take. Let's look at these two mind shifts.

The Past

We dwell on the past for various reasons. We may have good memories that are much better than our present situation. Maybe we just want those "good old days" back. Reminiscing is normal. Remembering the good times is healthy. *Living* in the past is unhealthy, for many reasons. It's when we *dwell* on our precious memories that we find ourselves stuck. Dwelling on the old days often (though not always) means that we are dissatisfied with the present state of our lives. Retreating to memories of days gone by indicates we are seeking comfort in what once was. At least that's one possible explanation. I'm not speaking of those people who are enjoying their memories. I'm talking about those who are literally reliving the good times. Everyone has encountered a person who only talks about the past and seems to remain unchanged over the years. These are the people whose minds are stuck in the past.

People will do this in their senior years, when they feel useless with nothing left to contribute to the world. In extreme cases, such as with Alzheimer's disease, an individual will allow a large portion of their consciousness to leave their bodies and relive those parts of their life again. This leaves their bodies in a zombie-like state with limited consciousness. This is nothing more than mental escapism.

One notable progression of this disease allows the person's consciousness to migrate to happier times. A person lives in relative happiness for many years, but an inner yearning calls them back. I have seen this for myself while working with Alzheimer's patients in hospice. You can sit next to them and know that their spirit has left their body. It's quite obvious that this person's body has been vacated. This is particularly true in the advanced stages of the disease.

There are other Alzheimer's mental states, in which the individual experiences other worlds and dimensions. I call this "straddling." Don't assume that a person's mind is no longer with them when they appear lifeless. They may actually be gaining great insight. We do this when we are sleeping. Consciousness is a lot like an iceberg; much of it exists below the surface.

Being stuck in the past because of guilt is even worse than reliving the good times. It's double trouble. Guilt keeps us stuck in the past, and creates a negative reality. You've probably heard the term "guilt trip." This is what it actually means. It's a trip into the past where we are invited to feel bad about ourselves. Guilt trips keep us from getting ahead. It's typical for people to dwell on everything they perceive as failures, rather than look at what was done well. It's clear that negative experiences carry more weight than the positive ones. This is true for most of us. We tend to call up our negative experiences more quickly than our memories of the good times. Maybe this is the perfectionist in us. We want to be right with the world. Guilt has some redeeming qualities for us. Guilt can teach something about the experiences we have had. Most of the time guilt informs us of what we should not do. It's good to know what not to do so that we can determine the right way of conducting ourselves.

We are constantly creating new pasts every time we choose a future possibility. Don't go away. Let me explain myself. This is true as every future has a long history behind it. When we choose a new path in the present moment, we accept the history behind it as well. The events that lead up to the probable future that becomes our reality will appear to have a chronological history that we have followed throughout our lives. I can assure you that this is not the case. In every moment that a new event manifests in our lives, it also brings a complete history. This history seems to be in line with the past we know because of the amnesia we agreed to before coming into this world. This phenomenon is necessary to the unfolding of the Master Plan and our functioning in the common reality. How could it be otherwise? The physical reality would not work for us if we knew the truth. Certainly not at this point in our development.

Let me give you a real life example of this concept from my career as a detective. I'm relating the story in simple terms because of the subject matter. A woman who harbored deep resentment toward her husband created a very serious situation involving her children. We'll say the oldest boy was eight and the youngest was four at the time of the incident. The youngest child told his mother that his father was seeing another woman. The oldest child confirmed this, stating that his father swore him to secrecy with bribes. This unfortunate situation is the result of the animosity between both parents. It will continue to grow as time goes by. Please understand me here, the mother is in no way responsible for this affair, and has a duty to protect her children.

What is important to this discussion is that when this matter came to the mother's attention, a whole history connected to the mistress came with it. The mistress's history came complete with stories and characters that attached themselves to the family's own history. This part of the story would be nonexistent if not for the original incident. That's right. Nonexistent.

When you select a future possibility, you accept all of the baggage that comes with it. Every time we have a thought, it branches out in infinite directions, in our reality and in others. These past events become part of our own history as if they have always been there. We do not know the difference. We go on with our lives as if nothing has changed. We build on them and make new choices based on those experiences. There is much more to life than we could imagine. I know this is confusing. Imagine what it must have been like for the Universal Architects to produce this particular effect. I wouldn't want that job.

Recently I found myself dwelling on an email I had sent out two months earlier. The message contained personal information that on reconsideration I decided should not have been released. I focused intently on this event for some time trying to come up with a way to contain the information. After a few hours, I checked Windows Mail and found that very email sitting in my draft folder undelivered. This is an example of how the mind can completely delete an event from a person's past. That email had already been sent and was on its way to creating its own trouble. Out of nowhere, the message appeared in an unsent folder where it had not been just an hour previous. That is excellent validation of the human potential. In the course of blocking that email from reaching its destination, the histories of unknown persons on the receiving end of that message never came to light.

The Role of Guilt

The kind of guilt that tells us we are "no good" and deflates our self-esteem is something to avoid. This unproductive guilt keeps us stuck in the past. Having guilt because you stole something is fine, and it's important. On the other hand, if you feel guilty because your child opted for an alternative lifestyle, you may be thinking about it the wrong way. When we feel guilty over what someone else did, it is usually false guilt. When we feel guilty for no good reason, we are impeding our personal growth. You cannot move on with your life when you dwell on what was. It is easier for a person to release true guilt than to overcome false guilt. And it's certainly easier to move on with one's life than to change the past. I'm certain it's possible to change your memories of the past, and therefore create a new (probable) future. If you are trapped by your past, it's crucial to your spiritual evolution that you get back on track.

I'm sure you've read about the "shoulda, coulda, woulda" syndrome in other books. If you haven't, I'm sure you've experienced it at some point in your life. That discouraged part of you that emerges and says, "If I could do it all over...," those are our regrets. These three words, "shoulda, coulda, woulda," also keep us from reaching our full potential. Regret is on a par with guilt. Regret has its roots in guilt. Unlike guilt, regret has little wisdom to offer us. For that reason, I have little use for it.

I would also like to touch on a forgotten emotion known as bitterness. This terrible emotion keeps us from maintaining relationships with those people we once held in high regard. Bitterness is the result of broken promises and disappointment. This is the result of one or more exchanges with a love gone sour. We find that we can no longer associate with the person we are angry with, so we choose to simmer for years on end. This sour attitude keeps us right where we are, mentally ensnared by the negative perception of past events that we refuse to release. This attitude works in the same way as regret and guilt, although its nature is somewhat different. Bitterness works not only against us in our physical world, but also in other realities. Bitterness is a profound state of isolation. We separate ourselves from others and the world. The bitter person mentally places himself or herself in other places and times. Others are unable to relate to the person in the common reality. This person is unreasonable and generally difficult to work with on a personal level.

The bitter person is stubborn and would much rather be right than continue with their evolution. You might hear a bitter person state, "We are never going to get along until you see things my way." The bitter person is in the same position as the zealot who denies any existence other than heaven, hell, and Earth. Both individuals are misguided and unyielding in their views. Both will experience little personal growth in this life. Flexibility is a positive attribute when it comes to personal growth. Rigidness puts us in a box. When this occurs, we believe that nothing exists outside the box. A more determined Christian will say, "It's not that you're wrong. It's that I'm right." I hope that line does not offend anyone. We should all be able to laugh at ourselves.

The Future

The future is not etched in stone. It is difficult to predict future events. A psychic cannot gaze into a crystal ball and accurately predict that certain events will come to pass. You will find that the unseen future remains closely tied to our present circumstances. Out of the infinite possible future realities that exist, some will become probabilities. These probable futures will eventually enter the present reality we know. A gifted psychic can pick up on these future probabilities. Mathematicians insist that they can reliably calculate the probability of both ordinary and extraordinary events. Math is not one of my strengths. There are many people belonging to Rosicrucian orders and other mystical groups that have a good handle on this. They seek to advance the spiritual development of our global community.

Possibilities and probabilities that do not manifest in this reality will appear in alternate realities, as real as the one in which you are now residing. For example, if your employer gives you the option of taking a management position in California, you have many possibilities before you. This goes beyond the simple yes or no scenario for which we generally take it. You might decide to look for another job. Perhaps you decide to look for another job within your profession. Alternatively, you may choose to start your own business. The possibilities are endless.

Out of the multitudes of possible realities, some are more likely to manifest. Some possibilities will become probabilities as we take action on them. Possibilities have consciousness and intelligence. They strive to become probabilities. The smallest action you take in any direction changes your reality. Change is a constant feature of human experience. The movements you make determine what comes next. This comes under the law of cause and effect. Your smallest action draws certain futures closer to you. It's unusual to perceive more than a few of these possibilities lining up. You should know that all future predictions you perceive, or receive from others, are probabilities. Don't get overly excited about any terrible circumstance in your life. You have the ability to change many of the things you are experiencing.

During our sleep cycle, we work with our teachers on creating the new day. The activities we intend to pursue and the challenges we choose to face are determined while we are sleeping. This always happens under the advice of those more experienced than ourselves, often in a classroom setting. It's not often that we make choices which further our spiritual evolution. Humans are known to take the easy way out. On the other hand, some of us put ourselves in the path of harm to learn a valuable lesson. We cannot specify the details of what will happen in the next day, nor can we control the external forces that affect us. We can only set the tone that our day will take. This is referred to as "reality mapping." Do not confuse this with any self-help or coaching technique.

You may be puzzled by the idea of living a future reality that has already occurred. If this aspect of the Master Plan were not true, psychics would not be able to receive future probabilities for others in "readings." If time is not an issue as I postulated, then the past, present, and future are not sequential and must therefore exist all at once.

Déjà vu is the experience of a specific probability materializing into your reality. This is a chosen future event becoming your present reality. You may have been aware of this future reality before it came into existence. The invisible world does not operate by clocks and calendars.

I'd like to point out that your past and future selves are able to contact you. Their messages may only be received by the subconscious mind, imperceptible to you yet quite powerful. Your future selves may warn you on specific actions to avoid and which ones to take. You will receive these messages as dreams, intuitions, visions, signs, and other subtle impressions. At other times, your higher power, the Universal Intelligence, guides, and deceased loved ones will send messages.

As for future escapism, people slip mentally into a future reality for reasons similar to those previously given. This may be an attempt to escape one's past or present due to less than desirable circumstances. Daydreamers or "reality escape artists" typically engage in this diversion. They have all kinds of thoughts about how their lives could be better. They dwell on what life would be like "if only" they could...get a better job, get a better education, meet their soul mate, move to Hawaii or play *Smoke on the Water* on the accordion.

In contrast, inspired thinkers are the kind of daydreamers that meditate on how to improve their lives and the lives of others. Society tends to confuse the two. Daydreaming to escape reality has the terrible effect of taking us away from what we need to be doing. Our journey comes to an abrupt halt when it takes us away from the present reality.

97

Planning is a safe way to prepare for a probable future while remaining grounded in the present. Planning enables us to take positive steps towards manifesting our visions, as opposed to daydreaming about what could be. However, it's imperative that we resist the human tendency to become absorbed in the details. People who plan often spend a considerable amount of time preparing for things that may never materialize. This activity can be exhausting. Planning every detail of our lives can overwhelm us. Don't get too far ahead of yourself. It's best to stay close to the present when making plans. Remember, the closer you are to the present moment the greater your chances are for your plans to unfold in this reality. The further out you go, the more possibilities there are.

For example, if you focus intently on getting your car fixed in the next three days, it's likely to happen. If you are saving for a house, your resolve could weaken due to various financial emergencies and changes in your living situation. The likelihood of this scenario becoming a reality also depends on your character. The point is that as the time between the present moment and your goal widens, the chances of the goal's emergence shrinks. Every thought manifests somewhere. There are infinite possibilities that compete with your designs. These mental competitors can interfere with the unfolding of your perfect plan. That doesn't mean you shouldn't save for a house or make plans for your summer vacation. I'm just bringing your attention to the mechanics behind this process.

The Universal Laws

The Seven Universal Laws

The universal laws explained in *The Kybalion*, a highly regarded metaphysical guide, apply to this reality and possibly others like it. There are other laws spoken of elsewhere that play a pivotal role in the workings of our reality, including basic physical laws such as Newton's universal gravitation and the three laws of motion. Our minds operate in a *conventional reality*. This term is similar to *common reality*, which I define as the conditions and arrangements that human beings collectively institute for experiencing a shared reality. I am speaking of the common attitudes and beliefs accepted by a people living together. It is out of necessity that our mental processes are attuned specifically to the common reality. If our minds were free to operate on any reality frequency, there would be no common reality; therefore, this human drama would never see a performance. Common reality in its simplest form is a consensus amongst society's members as to how various objects and situations should be recognized and communicated to each other. This includes definitions of words and symbols within a society or a section of society. This process is daunting. Ask any linguistics major.

I'd like to address *the seven universal laws,* as they are important to our understanding of the mechanics of the material world and the multiverse itself. I promise to discuss ideas that other authors would find unorthodox, even for metaphysics. That is how I do things. The seven universal laws originate in *the seven hermetic principles*, which can be found in the immutable *Kybalion*. *The Kybalion* was written in 1908 by an author who refers to him or herself, or themselves, as *The Three Initiates*. Some say *The Three Initiates* is a just a pen name. There is speculation that William Walker Atkinson wrote *The Kybalion*. The mystery has yet to be solved.

The principles set down in this classic metaphysical text are the words of wisdom handed down to us from Hermes Trismegistus. Trismegistus means "Trice-Great-Hermes." This legendary figure, deified in a number of ancient societies, has been associated with the Greek god Hermes, as well as the Egyptian god Thoth. Seekers of divine knowledge venerate Hermes Trismegistus for his mystical teachings. The metaphysical truths advanced by Hermes Trismegistus created what some have interpreted as a quasi-religious movement known as Hermeticism. Hermeticism, which can be traced back to Renaissance times, has contributed to notable accomplishments in modern times. I suggest following up on this reference to gain a better understanding of Hermeticism.

1. __The Law of Mentalism__

"Everything is mental; the universe is a mental creation of the all."

This principle asserts that the universe is mental. The LOM represents the truth regarding the nature of the multiverse. Everything that springs from the Universal Mind is mental. All creatures and structures are composed of mental energy. The very dimensions that contain our worlds are of a mental quality.

The LOM is absolute and immutable. We are able to manipulate the outcomes of some of these universal laws, including the laws of polarity and cause and effect. This fact is not true of the LOM.

Note that the LOM is inseparable from the laws of rhythm and vibration. The law of vibration expresses the existence of a fundamental unit of mental energy. The law of rhythm represents its movement and vitality. It is simple enough to say that they are the essence of mental energy.

This principle lets us know that mentalism is the name of the game. Mental "energy" serves as the structure physical reality. I say "energy" as there is no other general term to describe the mental characteristic of the universe. All things in the universe are mental constructs. The physical world is mental, although it may not appear that way to us. Our physical bodies are mental, as are our astral bodies, although they are of a different vibration. It's difficult to say whether consciousness is an energy, at least in the way we think of it. The Collective Consciousness states, "I am." There is no easy way of defining consciousness.

Why does this mental network exist? Our own domain exists as a complete mental framework designed to enable our physical experience. The entire system is meant to host our pursuit of spiritual evolution and perfection. You will note that spiritual evolution is referred to throughout this book, as it is a crucial point.

Because we are human, much of what and who God really is will remain a mystery to us until our departure from this reality. We can see the Divine's workings in the structures we are all too familiar with. From these objects, we base our knowledge of the Divine's mysterious presence. It is from our limited perception of the material landscape that the unknowable makes itself known – in as much as our minds can grasp. This statement doesn't apply to those highly respected religious leaders who have it all figured out. Of course, I'm not singling out one particular religion. It's a blanket statement.

2. <u>The Law of Correspondence</u>

"As above so below; as below so above; as within so without; as without so within."

The law of correspondence is arguably the most famous of the hermetic laws. I also feel that it is most mysterious and heretical in terms of its assertions about the nature of the universe. Out of this metaphysical rule comes the well-known mantra "As above, so below; as below, so above." What does this mean? My interpretation acknowledges a close relationship between the familiar outer world and the inner reality of which we are slowly becoming aware. I take it to mean that the universe as we know it has an exact equivalent on the other side. The LOC indicates that there is balance between both worlds. The Cosmic Mind assures us that whatever takes place on another plane will also materialize in this reality. The Christian saying "on Earth, as it is heaven" succinctly illustrates this principle. I have no knowledge of any similar sayings in other religions, but I'm sure there are.

The outer reality to which this principle refers can be defined as our perception of the physical environment. The outer reality is easy to identify. We have been discussing its nature throughout this book. We know physical reality very well since we participate in it. We play our various roles like actors in a motion picture. We walk around with amnesia, entering into one stimulating scene after another. However, few of us know the truth about our seemingly dense and unbroken environment.

It is difficult to define the inner world. However, the inner world is our connection to the multiverse. The inner world is the higher system to which I have been referring throughout this book. Our inner vision is our psychic access to existences in the restricted hidden universe. Through dreams, meditation, and other entry points, the invisible universe becomes plainly evident. With our inner resources, the curtains part so that we see the light. Then the truth is exposed.

The Law of Correspondence is the counterpart of the creative and industrious law of attraction. The LOA is an action that allows thoughts to manifest into physical reality, thereby ensuring universal harmony. This means that all mental concepts will physically appear in this reality or another. The LOC specifies that there is a corresponding relationship between the internal and external realities. Whatever you feel on the inside will manifest on the outside. This function is carried out by the LOA.

Like many of the hermetic laws, the LOC shows itself to have a necessary mutual relationship with the LOA. The LOC is the universal principle that specifies that if you are miserable on the inside, you will be miserable on the outside. This is true if you suffer from chronic depression. The illness will be visible in your character as well as in your appearance. Others will see you as you feel. Things will be difficult for you. If you experience joy, this feeling will be reflected in your outer world. You have a pleasant experience. In conjunction with the LOA, your internal thoughts will materialize in the external world just as Law of Attraction coaches teach. The thought forms you create on the other side will produce an equivalent physical form in the common reality. As above, so below. If you create a thought that your boss will reprimand you for being late for work, he will. If you have a consistent thought pattern that you will achieve great things in life, you certainly will.

Like the Law of Mentalism, the LOC is absolute. This principle does nothing less than ensure a balance between both worlds. It does so without fail. You cannot defy universal laws. If such laws could be interrupted, the structure of reality would collapse upon itself. By understanding the universal laws and working with them, you can experience a more fulfilling life. Your success in this reality is entirely dependent upon your proficiency with these laws.

3. **The Law of Vibration**

"Nothing rests; everything moves; everything vibrates."

This principle is scientifically unproven, yet completely accurate. The world is filled with mental structures of every size and shape. We should wonder why most of us are able to think clearly. There's way too much commotion going on. It's a good thing we're able to tune out much of it.

Have you ever heard someone say they got a good or bad vibe from a certain person? This happens when a person's inner senses are noticing the vibratory nature of a person, place, or situation. Our universe is permeated with vibrations. Again, our reception of these vibrations is limited. There are reasons for this. If we were able to perceive what exists beyond objective reality, the illusion would break and the master plan would unravel.

Higher knowledge is considered sacred and not easy to acquire. The masses go about their business in a daze. This is how it has been from the beginning. However, what the privileged few know, the rest will eventually learn. Someday soon an awakening will occur. I believe it is our destiny. Ignorance is not conducive to the survival of a race.

The underlying substance of the physical universe consists of this vibratory energy. Every square inch of space is filled with a network of vibrations. Even thought is a type of vibration. According to Buick (GM), each person has three thousand thoughts a day. If that is the case, then the world must be inundated with vibrations. To my knowledge, mental transmissions do not dissipate over time. They are not degradable. I understand (intuitively) that they are able to occupy the same space without causing congestion.

Each vibration does a specific job, just as a human cell is assigned to a particular body system. For example, there is a certain vibratory frequency for wood and another for metal. What is vibrational energy? Well, energy is a very vague term in this business. People use the word energy to describe all sorts of physical and nonphysical manifestations. Like most people, I tend to use the word energy liberally. If vibrations are the most basic and universal energy, then all things must exist as energy.

We experience vibrations through our five senses and through extrasensory perception. Substantiating the existence of a vibrational structure for a physical object would require advanced technology not available to us in this age. Nor do I believe it is necessary. Our sixth sense makes it possible to distinguish those frequencies not accessible by our physical senses. Under the right circumstances, you may be able to see this vibrational energy. An exercise to do this is included elsewhere in this book.

Validating the existence of an omnipresent vibrational energy would not bring humankind any closer to a mass awakening. We are already aware of the atomic structure of the physical world. That hasn't gotten us very far in terms of our spiritual evolution. We need to search within for the answers, not by using our physical senses.

Keeping all that in mind, without our bodies we would not be able to experience this life. The human body is the key here. Our bodies keep us from receiving information from the other side. Our ability to perceive other realities is hindered and all but cut off by the flesh. You see, everything exists as frequencies. Every particle vibrates and has a slightly different frequency. You can see this for yourself when you change radio stations. Any particular station has a distinct signal. There are specific vibrations for each molecular combination. This is true of liquids, solids, gases, light, and all things.

The vibrational energy takes on the appearance of atoms, which are the building blocks of the material world. This should not surprise anyone with even a little knowledge of physics. Most of you probably know more about the physical sciences than I do. My contention is that all vibrations would appear the same, if not for the law of rhythm, which determines their cyclical rate. Things could not be distinguished and would, therefore, be unintelligible. The fact that atoms boil down to vibrational energy is all you really need to know. You will find good information on the metaphysical nature of vibrational energy if you look in the right places. The Internet is one place to look.

Just as a refresher, there are two schools of thought on the nature of energy and its relationship to the universe. The first is dualism. This is the theory that there are two kinds of universal energy and material. Philosophers have chosen to attribute one of these two energies to mental phenomena. In ages past, people called this mysterious energy vital fluid. Vital fluid keeps all living creatures alive. The other energy is reserved for physical objects.

The other theory is called *monism*. This is the idea that one energy occupies the entire universe. I like to compare the Christian concept of the Holy Ghost (the breath of God) with monism. Unfortunately, monism and dualism take one into a deep philosophical discussion, which I cannot adequately cover in this book.

Another subject I feel is worth visiting involves the idea of dark matter. This is an invisible force that scientists believe makes up 83% of the matter of the universe. The dark matter theory was proposed by Fritz Zwicky in the 1930s.[2] Though government agencies, universities, and independent research facilities have poured millions of dollars into the search for dark matter, this undefined, mysterious force remains undetectable. I think scientists are going in the wrong direction with their investigation. An examination of our existing belief systems may provide the answers we seek. There's a possible link between dark matter and the belief in energies such as chi, ki, Prana, the vital fluid, Reiki, and orgone that certain societies say pervade the universe. Although I cannot qualify this notion, there are probably thousands of intelligent and rational people who agree with this premise.

There exists an unspoken relationship between metaphysics and physics, even though most scientists say that the two are wholly unrelated. I am not sure how one would go about tying dark matter to a vital life force, but it seems like a worthwhile venture. Dark matter cannot be substantiated any more than a universal life force can be proven to exist. I do understand the resistance to a metaphysical approach since it flies in the face of inflexible standards created by modern science.

---

[2] Wikipedia, *Dark Matter,* http://en.wikipedia.org/wiki/Dark_matter, accessed May 27, 2012.

Recently I was able to see puffs of the dark matter in a darkened room. It had the appearance of an inky, cloudy substance. It had no discernible form. This dark matter is easier to detect indoors than in open areas. One must possess an inner awareness and a determination to witness it. I can assure you, it is not a hallucination. This isn't like the *Grudge* or some other horror movie. It may be frightening if you do not understand it. Exposure to this sort of phenomenon will help you to develop a tolerance for and eventual familiarity with the supernatural. I still struggle with it at times.

4. <u>The Law of Polarity</u>

"Everything is dual; everything has poles; everything has its pair of opposites that are identical in nature, but different in degrees; extremes meet; all truths are but half-truths."

Polarity is a universal duality theory. This principle supports the idea that everything has its opposite. The law of polarity explains the apparent order and chaos of the world. It is the separation between this world and the next. There are thousands of known dualities in the physical world. Here are some of these:

- Good and evil
- Dark and light
- Hot and cold
- Fast and slow
- Positive and negative
- Happy and sad
- Hard and soft

- Beautiful and ugly
- Fat and skinny
- Abundant and scarce

And the list goes on.

It's important to note that there are no dualities on the other side, although other physical realities may use the principles of the LOP. The LOP is essential to our functioning at this stage of human development. Duality makes the illusion of our physical system seem real. We have a psychological need to make comparisons. We could never think of abandoning our labels. This would force us to accept things as they are, including other people. This isn't meant to say that all people are the same. It just means that people are people. Remember the God of the Old Testament saying, "I am." This is the existence to which we should aspire. Through the reincarnational process, we will eventually reach a more enlightened state of being.

People choose to see dualities incrementally as you would on a thermometer. For example, there are two faucets, one for hot water and another for cold. We normally turn the cold on and slowly add the hot water until it gets to the temperature we want. Therefore, hot and cold give the impression of being polar opposites. We see these extremes moving away from each other in degrees. This is reasonable. In truth, these opposing temperatures come together so that we observe their flow as a continuum. There are no extremes, degrees, or dualities. The LOP exists as an infinite continuum with no beginning or end. The universe flows. There are no labels. That is a human practice.

There is no absolute evil or good. This is true because there is no way to measure it. You could say that premeditated murder is a heinous offense. It's worse than manslaughter. However, what is worse than premeditated murder? Maybe a murder involving torture. What could be worse than that? To determine this, one would have to explore his or her own belief system, or ask for someone else's opinion. I realize this illustration is a bit macabre. I draw from my experiences. My intention is to show that dualities are merely opinions. A person might try to put his or her finger on a particular attribute of an object and say: "This flower is ugly, but this one is attractive." First, these judgments are subjective. Neither flower can be marked ugly or attractive. Objectivity is also opinion, since everyone describes reality differently.

Marathons are interesting to observe from a duality perspective. Whenever a runner breaks a record, people say, "No one will ever break the runner's time. That is the fastest a person can run." Yet the record is then consistently broken. How is that possible? The LOP is not subject to our self-imposed limitations.

The list below describes both the perception and truth of the law of polarity:

- There are no absolutes in physical reality.
- Duality is a contradiction in terms.
- The extremes exist on the same pole.
- Polarity is a seamless continuum.
- Opposites are equal in nature.

In America, we say, "there are two sides to every story." Broadly interpreted, this means that each person has his or her own perception of an object or situation. Two people can look at the same object or situation and come up with two different interpretations or descriptions for it. I'm going to propose that you perform the following experiment:

You should obtain the assistance of an open-minded friend for this. Find an empty soda can and crush it a little. Ask your friend to describe the can in writing. He or she should describe the colors, shape, texture, size, weight, aesthetic impression, usefulness, etc. Then you would proceed to do the same. You will be amazed at the difference in interpretation. The words used to describe the various aspects of the can may be closely related or vastly different, but it shows that people have their own way of examining the world. This process will clearly demonstrate the extremes of the LOP. The results will clue you in to your own reality.

In my career as a private investigator, I spent a considerable amount of my time working for criminal defense attorneys. One of my responsibilities involved taking statements from witnesses. I carefully analyzed what the witnesses related regarding the crime. This is exactly the purpose of the soda can experiment. It raises awareness and teaches us to make a reliable interpretation of the information we are receiving.

When I interviewed several witnesses to a crime, each person would provide different versions of the incident. That is the nature of personal reality. Each person experiences the same event in his or her own way. It is extremely difficult to obtain an accurate account of what occurred in any particular situation. I found this to be especially true when witnesses attempted to describe an unknown suspect fleeing the scene. Certain details always match, but their versions can vary greatly. People tend to be more subjective than objective in their answers. People are not choosy with their words.

This unique view of the interpretation process is the essence of the law of polarity. It's quite obvious when two people have opposite views; it's also apparent at every point in between these two extremes. Of course, there are no real points of reference.

5. <u>The Law of Rhythm</u>

"Everything flows out and in; everything has its tides; all things rise and fall; the pendulum-swing manifests in everything; the measure of the swing to the right is the measure of the swing to the left; rhythm compensates."

The universe is an ocean of vibrational energy faithfully maintaining its rhythmical flow to all its parts. As I mentioned previously, in this book the Law of Rhythm works as one with the Law of Vibration. Without the Law of Vibration, we would not have the Law of Rhythm. The rate of vibration determines the design of the material things we are familiar with, and possibly those nonphysical things we do not yet know. I believe that the fundamental laws, including the LOV, apply to the entire multiverse.

Rhythm would not happen if it were not for what I call the "space in between." This situation has to do with the spaces between the vibrations. This is a concept that I became aware of in the 1990s. It may be written about elsewhere, but it's an important subtopic to this discussion. These spaces are just as important as the material that comes before and after them. You can see this in musical notes. There can be no song or composition without the spaces. The spaces are something – not nothing. They are a key feature of the physical world.

I'd like to offer you a real life application of the space in between. Let me assure you that what you leave out is as important as what you put in. For example, let's say that what you don't do is an achievement in itself. When communicating with another person, keeping your mouth closed is sometimes the best policy. I'm sure we can all relate to that. We've all had those moments when we've put our foot in our mouth and said something we've regretted.

When I was eighteen, my father encouraged me to join the auxiliary police in my hometown. My father was a sergeant in the unit for many years. I was often assigned to traffic duty for special events. I would get right out into the middle of traffic to direct it. At times, this created unnecessary frustration for the drivers. My father told me to leave the traffic alone as it would take care of itself, especially at certain times of the day. My point is, sometimes it is better to do nothing and let things happen. Nothingness can be a blessing.

The "space in between" theory has potential applications in areas not yet conceived by modern science. Perhaps the spaces are a means for interdimensional travel. We can already do this in our nonphysical bodies, but there are places in the multiverse that require unique entry methods. I only have a slight sense of what this could mean for the development of humankind. These applications will reveal themselves only when we are ready to receive them. We cannot fathom what the Universal Mind has in store for us.

The body has its own rhythms. Aptly enough, they are called biorhythms. The biorhythms I am speaking of should not be confused with the kind having to do with astrology and numerology. Through biorhythms, a person's physical, mental, and emotional cycles can be determined. Professionals refer to biorhythms as circadian rhythms. Circadian rhythms are the cycles of body functions, such as sleep, hormone release, and body temperature. Chronobiology is the study of circadian rhythms. Circadian rhythm research has traditionally focused on sleep and the correction of sleep disorders. Much research has been done to uncover the secrets of sleep. Researchers contend that we possess a "master clock" in the hypothalamus called the suprachiasmatic nucleus (SCN). The SCN regulates a number of tinier clocks spread throughout the body. These clocks are meant to be in sync at all times. [3]

There are also body rhythms that are given far less attention than that of sleep, including digestion and aging. I have noticed that at certain intervals, I'll lose two pounds, and then my weight will go up two pounds. I've found that even if I eat nothing, I will still gain the two pounds, and it will stay that way until the next cycle. I am guessing that small gains and losses have little to do with our eating habits. Perhaps even larger weight gains have something to do with circadian rhythms. How many of you are aware of digestive cycles? Whether you are healthy or ill, you may see a pattern in your lavatory visits. You may discover patterns that require your attention as a matter of good health. I am not afraid to break etiquette when duty calls.

It's been claimed by a number of groups that humans generate a completely new body every seven years. This is because millions of cells die and are born every day. I am confident that this theory will stand up to hard skepticism in the end. Some scientists say that different cells have

---

[3] National Institutes of Health/National Institute of General Medical Sciences, *Circadian Rhythms Fact Sheet*, nigms.hih.gov, http://www.nigms.nih.gov/Education/Factsheet_CircadianRhythms.htm, accessed April 23, 2011.

different life cycles and some cells, such as neurons, do not regenerate. I do not accept this last piece of information.

When the body's rhythms experience a sudden interruption, problems are sure to emerge. This is especially true when we react to stressful events. Acute stress throws the body out of whack. The internal rhythms of our systems and organs lose their balance. The sensitive vibrations of which our systems are composed cannot maintain homeostasis. This causes all manner of physical maladies. For example, a heart rhythm disorder is referred to as arrhythmia. In other instances of rhythmic "skipping" you might encounter diseases like ulcerative colitis and Crohn's disease. Disruptions in other body networks such as the respiratory system may create medical conditions such as pneumonia. More often than not, psychological stress is the precipitating factor leading to such conditions. This scenario takes place in all organs and systems of the body.

Scientists have found that all living creatures have these rhythms, including plants and tiny microbes. It's safe to say that all material things possess unique rhythms. In fact, even the nonphysical universe has rhythm. Scientists are slowly becoming aware of the law of rhythm, its design, and mechanisms. What these diligent researchers fail to grasp is that this principle draws its power from the Universal Source from which all vibrational rhythms originate. The Universal Source acts as the central clock synchronizing the rhythm radiating from every part of creation. According to the philosophy of *panpsychism*, all things have some form of consciousness. The LOR makes it clear that all animate or inanimate entities possess a distinct vibrational rhythm. By maintaining vibrational stability, these entities are able to maintain a harmonious relationship with the Divine Consciousness.

If you are acquainted with circadian body rhythms, then you might also be familiar with human brain wave research. In 1908, Dr. Hans Berger, an Austrian psychiatrist, unlocked the door to our true potential by uncovering the presence of electrical activity in the human brain. Of course, this condition already existed, but the fact that we are aware it changes our opinion about what is possible in human potential. Dr. Berger referred to these frequencies as alpha brainwaves, as they were the first waves to be documented. Additionally, Dr. Berger is credited with inventing the electroencephalograph (EEG). The purpose of this device is to record and graph the electrical activities in the brain. In later years, researchers discovered other types of brainwaves including beta, theta, and delta. Here is a description of these frequencies:

Beta – This is the normal waking state. In the beta state, our awareness is focused on physical reality. Beta waves range between 13 to 30 cycles (Hz).

Alpha – We achieve this state when we are mentally relaxed. We are typically in the alpha state when our eyes are closed. Alpha waves range between 8 to 13 Hz.

Theta – This state is associated with deep relaxation, meditation, the early stages of sleep, daydreaming, and creativity. This is a highly desirable state for those exploring consciousness. Theta waves range between 4 to 7 Hz.

Delta – These frequencies are generally seen in an unconscious person, especially during sleep and catalepsy. Delta waves range between 1 to 4 Hz.

This discovery is valuable as a means of identifying and measuring states of consciousness. This method has no great significance outside of the physical realm. Science is foremost an exploration of the material world. The cycles and phases of the mind as we understand them are not representative of its true nature. It is impossible to analyze consciousness using physical ideas and methods. Could you use a Slinky to make a complicated weather forecast? This comparison is obviously absurd, and that is my point. Still, this approach gives us a way of penetrating the indefinable nature of the universe. It's a starting point.

Certain mental exercises such as meditation, deep relaxation, and hypnotic states access hidden layers of consciousness. The nature of these techniques is very similar and leads to the same outcome. I regularly practice meditation for thirty minutes a day. I am also a certified hypnotist. I like to practice meditation to quiet my thoughts and to relax. I also use it for a few seconds or minutes during the day to clear my thoughts. Meditation allows us to slow down our racing thoughts. These incessant mental intrusions can overwhelm us when we focus too intently on what is going on in our immediate environment. This is how stress forms. At such times, our thoughts create a sense of urgency and demand our attention. Short periods of meditation can give us an opportunity to reassess the reality of our situation. Longer meditation periods can be a time of reflection to determine what is important to us. Here are some benefits of meditation:

- Helps us gain clarity
- Produces profound visions
- Acts as an aid for relaxation
- Provides access to intuition and inner resources

- Stirs up our creativity and insight
- Allows us to reflect on our short term and long term progress
- Enables us to connect with the Infinite for a brief period

Meditation conjures up images of sitting cross-legged in a temple or on a remote mountaintop contemplating the meaning of life. I will tell you that meditation is possible anywhere. You can even meditate during a coffee break in your little cubicle if you have one. You will find meditation has benefits not found in a cup of coffee. Many people find it refreshing to close their eyes briefly at long traffic lights. Just don't get the people behind you irritated. This kind of light meditation produces a shift in consciousness that causes a person to enter the alpha state. This level provides access to our intuitive side and a heightened sense of awareness.

After a while, meditation will become a routine – just like making the bed. If making your bed doesn't appeal to you, don't worry – meditation is much more enjoyable. I feel agitated when I don't get my down time. I wonder why I feel that way, and then I realize that I was running around so much that I forgot to meditate. I have had insomnia because of this.

Interestingly, I have heard that a thirty-minute meditation period is equal to about four to five hours of sleep. I imagine the ratio depends on who you ask. I do not believe a deep meditation provides the same benefits as sound sleep. The qualities of each are distinct. Firstly, meditation takes place in the alpha/theta range, whereas sleep occurs in the delta. Meditation serves a different purpose from sleep. Important events and processes take place in the sleep cycle. There are certain forms of instruction and training which take place on other levels of reality to help us successfully navigate physical life. Problem solving and planning are a big part of this cycle. With that in mind, meditation is an excellent complement to your good sleep-time habits. Keeping a relaxation routine makes our sleep activities more productive.

At some point during my meditations, I notice that my consciousness dips or shifts into a different kind of focus. I can only describe this state by saying that something about it feels different. At these times, I notice that something in my awareness has changed. It's like being in one state of mind and then moving to another. It's not a "feeling" *per se*. It's recognized by your internal senses. This inner feeling receives information that is very different from the signals you receive through your five physical senses. We use these senses to track fluctuations in consciousness. The awareness I am speaking of came to me after practicing twenty or thirty minutes every day for over a year. This example is representative of only one of the many observations that you will make in your own exploration of consciousness. You will experience many unexplainable events in the study of consciousness. The majority of these remarkable explorations go unreported because there is no way to translate what the observer has experienced. The reason for this is that consciousness is a personal journey. The knowledge that one receives in dreams, meditation, and out-of-body experiences is solely for that person. Reading a book on this topic gets you motivated and gives you some understanding, but you must undertake your own investigation to learn firsthand what exists beyond the psychic wall.

Incidentally, the word psychic is not my favorite term for describing anything related to metaphysics or consciousness. I say this because of its misuse. The same is true of the words soul, astral, and spiritual. These words are broadly used and have too many meanings. Our society is inadvertently perverting its most useful words, at least in American literature.

Now that I've finished my meanderings on meditation, I'd like to point out that there are much larger rhythms in the universe. Some of these rhythms originate within the Earth itself. We have identified many Earth cycles, including the water, carbon, and nitrogen.

There are rhythmical cycles beyond our planet. One is the lunar cycle. Here, we are concerned with the moon's orbit around the Earth, which is 27.3 days. The lunar cycle produces the high and low tides. The tides help organisms in their journeys. Some organisms ride with the high tide while others move in tandem with the low tide. Lunar rhythms have many apparent correlations to the cycles in nature. There are studies linking the lunar phases with the menstrual cycle and fertility.

Let's not forget the solar cycles, which govern the solstices and equinoxes, as well as influencing weather patterns. There are even greater rhythms that we cannot perceive, including that of the universe itself. There may well be nonphysical rhythms beyond our current understanding.

On a less serious note, there are some notable musicians from years gone by who spoke of rhythm in inanimate objects and ideas. In the song, "Year of the Cat" by Al Stewart, released in 1976, Stewart sings of "the rhythm of the newborn day." This song has been my favorite song since I was a child. The year of the cat is part of the Vietnamese calendar, which cycles every twelve years. This zodiac animal symbolizes a time of great change. We have seen incredible suffering across the globe in the form of political discontent, economic ruin, and social disintegration. This may be the movement of the mass consciousness in a new direction. Upheaval is usually a precursor to an awakening or a new way of thinking.

Artists in particular are sensitive to the rhythms of the universe. A number of prominent musicians wrote about the "Rhythm of Love," including the Plain White Ts. Then of course, there is the "Rhythm of the Falling Rain," by The Cascades in 1962. Rod Stewart has the "Rhythm of My Heart." I also remember Debarge's "Rhythm of the Night," which came out in 1985. I could list many more examples, but you get the idea.

6. <u>The Law of Cause and Effect</u>

"Every cause has its effect; every effect has its cause; everything happens according to the law; chance is but the name for a law not recognized; there are many planes of causation, but nothing escapes the law."

There are some implications of our thoughts producing activity that we need to be aware of. Any decisions we make or don't make affect not only our family and friends, but also other people with whom we are associated. You see, cause and effect has a reciprocal relationship. An effect appears every time a thought or action takes place – without fail. For example, when water is poured on a fire, it is quickly extinguished. The extinguished fire is the effect. The water poured on the fire is the cause. The chain of cause and effect is extensive and complex. I will take this up a notch and suggest that the water poured on the fire was also an effect, since the person that poured the water was the cause of that action. One thing leads to another. Each action you take leads to endless possible future events. This is where people have proposed theories about how a man sneezing in San Diego could trigger a chain of events which leads to a massive tsunami in Indonesia. We do not know what our actions hold for our neighbors. I do agree that our thoughts have widespread effects on the rest of the world, however big or small.

Let's look at a positive example of this principle. Let's say that you are walking down a typical busy street on an ordinary day. As you make your way down the street, you see an ordinary-looking man (a woman would work just as well) approaching you with a dejected look on his face. He looks up at you for a moment. Instead of turning away, you smile cheerily at the sad man and continue on your way, thinking nothing more of it. What you didn't know is that this man was having the worst day of his life, and was contemplating suicide. Your bright smile made the desperate soul forget all about his misery and suicidal thoughts. In fact, the man was so inspired that the next day he took steps to clean up his life. The following year he applied to law school. He graduated in the top of his class. He went on to become a district attorney and helped take dangerous criminals off the streets. Later in his career, he became a highly regarded politician and helped save lives throughout the world. How is that for cause and effect? I'll bet you never realized how far a warm smile could go. This scenario is certainly possible. Again, we do not know the implications of our thoughts and actions. This law is impressive in its power.

In most cases, the cause of a particular matter can usually be traced back to you. We all bear some responsibility for what happens to us. Personal responsibility is a strict rule for law of attraction practitioners (attractionists). It is also a very bold and controversial statement. No one wants to believe that he or she is the cause of his or her own happiness and misery. This would mean that people have a degree of control over their lives. Isn't it much easier to blame others for our failures, losses, and heartaches? I'm not going to debate the amount of control we actually have over our experiences. Some would argue that nothing *happens* to us since we are the responsible party. Attractionists insist we initiate the events through our thoughts.

We should all agree that there are no simple answers. Many contributing factors lead to a particular result. Some reasons are quite apparent while others require a bit of thinking. I do know that when we recognize our role for the life we have created, we are able to use the law of cause and effect to influence the direction it takes. One way to create favorable outcomes is to think before you act. Have a game plan. Don't just react to situations. Think about what you are going to do in a situation *before* you move to take action.

The LOCE reinforces my position that we live in an orderly universe. When we accept the idea that one event leads directly to another, it eliminates the need to believe in luck, coincidences, and accidents. Clearly, there are no accidents when one can trace an effect back to its cause. The allure of a random universe vanishes when we realize that everything happens for a reason. Some of us believe in the illusion of randomness to avoid facing the truth. The LOCE presents things as they are. It does not pull punches. The LOCE just gives the facts. This is not necessarily a bad thing. If you will learn to work with the LOCE and the other universal laws mentioned in this book, your success is assured. Just a willingness to accept this principle (the cause) will put you on a path to a brighter future (the effect).

I should mention that this principle is associated with karma. The idea of receiving punishment in successive incarnations for wrongs we have committed in the present life does not sit well with me. Although I will not pretend to be knowledgeable of the concept of karma, I cannot accept the idea of reincarnational debt. I choose the natural consequences of this world over reincarnational debt and eternal damnation. What is your preference?

7. <u>The Law of Gender (also called the Law of Gestation or Generation)</u>:

"Gender is in everything; everything has its masculine and feminine principles; gender manifests on all planes."

This law specifies that humans possess both male and female characteristics. In other words, we have a male side and a female side. The fact is that a human is gender neutral. In each of our incarnations, we take on a male or female persona. We have all been both male and female in our many past lives. Some people hold on tightly to the gender of their most recent past life. Those who do this find themselves unable to give up the identity, for whatever reason. When this occurs, homosexuality appears. In light of this, it's entirely possible to conclude that gay people are born that way. That doesn't mean we are obligated to take on a homosexual role. As I stated, a human being is gender neutral. Gender is the earthly design of the universal mind. Within all of us are the memories of each of our past lives. Therefore, we all possess male and female qualities. For the most part, masculine and feminine qualities follow an individual's physical attributes. Some of us show strong qualities of the opposite sex, while maintaining the given gender. For example, some men

126

show their feelings and some women are aggressive. These are the masculine and feminine traits that each of us display from time to time. I know this information is offensive to some people, but metaphysics itself is a controversial subject.

A number of old sayings allude to the esoteric mean ing of the law of gender. Here are a few:

"Everything comes in time." --Rabelais

"Everything comes if a man will only wait."--Disraeli

"All things come round to him, who will but wait."-- Longfellow

"There's a time for everything." --Mark Price

"All in due time" or "It will happen when it's sup posed to happen." - - English saying

"All good things come to he who waits." --English saying

Though authors were unable to articulate what these adages meant in technical terms, they were trying to express the idea that a certain amount of time must pass before our thoughts manifest into reality. It's much like the germination period of a seed, or the process of fetal development in humans. Keep in mind that there are feminine and masculine forces at work in both cases. The LOG works in tandem with the law of rhythm. In modern times, we understand that time exists between the completions of cycles. We see this in the natural cycles of the universe such as the Earth, which makes a complete rotation in approximately 23 hrs and 56 minutes, and a 365.25 day revolution around the sun. This simple progression is evident in the amount of time it takes to get from the beginning of a cycle to the end. In other words, we experience time as a cycle that comes full circle.

Other insightful writers trying to make sense of the LOG have likened it to the gestation period of a plant. They explain it in terms of the time a seed must take to grow into its intended form.

Humans have great difficulty with the LOG. The adages I referred to before all convey a common idea. That is the patience we must have to see our creations and those of the universe reach their full potential. By this, I mean that the time it takes for our plans to come to fruition. Many of us have an unusual aversion to the timeless nature of the LOG. You can certainly see it in the over-indulging materialists who expect to get their desires fulfilled immediately. It's a condition of the modern world. Although not everyone who is overly impatient is a hedonist.

Our needs do not impede our spiritual progress in this life. However, other impediments such as impatience cause us one setback after another. Some of you may be familiar with the saying, "God works in his own time," or something similar to that. As I mentioned in the section on time, the universe operates outside of this conventional system. Physical laws do not apply to the Universal Mind. We cannot force our beliefs on the source. Until we understand this law, we may experience eternal disappointment with the speed at which things seem to move for us. When we learn patience, we can finally be at peace with cosmic laws enacted by the Collective Consciousness.

Law of Attraction

This is not one of the hermetic principles. So much attention has been given to the Law of Attraction these days that I feel compelled to put my two cents in. The LOA is actually a union of the seven hermetic principles. In other words, they are the working components of the LOA. This a loaded statement. There is great debate over what the actual mechanism of the LOA is. My theory represents but one thought on the matter. I'm not going to rehash the same old LOA theories other writers have thoroughly covered in their books. I want to examine some less-considered items relating to this principle.

The LOA ensures us that whatever we think *will* manifest in the physical reality either immediately or at an appointed time. This will happen every time without fail just as attractionists tell us. For instance, when you think of a green tennis ball, you create the precise quality of energy to form an actual green tennis ball. The ball will materialize in the exact size, shade, weight, and consistency you specify. This will happen whether or not you are conscious of these details. Your subconscious may take the specifics from an early memory you have of a green tennis ball. The mental energy used to create the ball will electromagnetically (for lack of a better term) attract the atoms to it. The atoms will "stick" to the thought form with the help of universal forces. The atoms will proceed to fill it in by positioning themselves in a way that makes the green tennis ball physically appear. This process takes place on a vibratory level which we cannot perceive. If the thought form is a situation that needs to be played out, the mental energy of which I speak will set things in motion. These events will occur in their own time, since time and space do not exist outside of this reality. This is a simplified explanation of a highly complex system. I'd like to give this process the name "fulfillment," a term my Christian friend uses to describe his relationship with Jesus. Those souls brave enough to adopt this theory will find themselves sufficiently humbled before the Great Architect.

You cannot perceive a thought form with your five senses. These are one of the many human limitations. The energetic forms we generate are perfect in every way. They exist in the same room with you, but not in your reality. Thought forms can appear in any location. They can be anywhere in this world or in another. It depends on the intensity and nature of the thought energy that created it. There are many reasons why thought forms materialize on another plane. On a deeper level of consciousness (subconscious), you may be assisting someone else or even a remote society with their mission. You may only discover these truths in dreams or meditation.

One point that is typically left out of most LOA manuals is that this principle operates in many other realities. While this is a deeply metaphysical matter, it's worth delving into briefly for no other reason than to acquire higher knowledge. Every thought will not only materialize in this reality, but also in an endless number of alternate universes. Life is full of possibilities. Infinite possibilities would be a correct statement. We see them as choices. Here is an example. You are planning your annual vacation and you have narrowed it down to three different locations: Orlando, Las Vegas, and Myrtle Beach. As you consider these vacation spots, you envision yourself at each one of them, having the time of your life. Your mind is overcome by feelings of excitement. Finally, you decide on Vegas. This decision becomes a probability. You do, in fact, go to Vegas and have an amazing time. Now, by going to Vegas you have eliminated Myrtle Beach and Orlando as contenders for your annual vacation. These possibilities all but vanish from your conscious mind. However, the thoughts you have created do not dissipate. If they do not material-ize physically on this plane, they will certainly go on to manifest in an alternate reality. These other vacation pos-sibilities will go on to play themselves out in an alternate reality just as if you had gone to Orlando and Myrtle Beach rather than Las Vegas. Another "you," an alter ego, will live out these scenarios. This other you is just as real and as physical as you are yourself. And like you, this alter ego believes himself to be the only one that exists. None of you would be likely to have any knowledge of each other. This view of the Law of Attraction is definitely more ar-cane than the principle itself. Despite this, I find that this idea fills in some of the holes left unfilled by LOA theo-rists.

I use the term "alternate reality" to describe a parallel universe. The terms "alternate reality" and "alternate di-mension" have a different meaning in science fiction lit-erature. Some popular movies that depict alternate realities include *It's a Wonderful Life* starring James Stewart and *Back to the Future II* with Michael J. Fox. Alternate reali-ties are a commonly used theme in motion pictures. People enjoy playing "What if?"

The upside and downside of this alternate reality business is that anything your alter ego(s) conjures up in his or her mind may manifest in this reality. Therefore, if your alter ego considers entering the military, but instead goes to college, you may receive a telepathic suggestion to enlist. Don't forget, there are many other alternative fu-tures that may insert themselves into your life path, de-pending upon the choices you make. This knowledge should give you a new perspective on the role you play in shaping your outcomes. This is especially true when it comes to understanding those less than favorable events. Then again, this information may not be very comforting.

To conceptualize the idea of infinite realities, I refer you to the following experiment I learned when I was a child. Just hold a smaller mirror up to a bigger mirror. You will see the smaller mirror you are holding up in the big mirror. Look into the reflection of the smaller mirror. If you look at it from the right angle, you will notice a series of mirrors like a long deck of cards spreading out into infinity. That is the idea of possible futures.

Our thought-generating behavior affects not only people we have contact with in this reality (like our friends and family), but also people residing in alternate dimensions. Because the LOA is absolute and will always deliver, we must be careful with our thoughts. This is a good example of thought control. Some are able to "watch what they say," but few of us are able to rein in our ego by being mindful. This is a lifelong pursuit. It takes a strong awareness of one's self to attain any level of proficiency. I do feel that mastery of one's conscious mind will be a characteristic of future civilizations. We're not ready for it at this time. Most of us are barely even aware that we exist as eternal beings. In the meantime, it's fair to say that we are all mental polluters, in the sense that we are not aware of the thoughts we generate.

One school of thought asserts, like law of attraction practitioners, that we are responsible for *everything* we experience. Attractionists state that we attract people, objects, and situations into our lives. If this is true, it is also possible that everything we experience is part of a reality we are responsible for manufacturing. I mean the entire landscape including the trees, rocks, and even the stars, as well as the planet beneath our feet. It would be like participating in a virtual reality game in which we mentally construct all of the scenes. This view is from a branch of philosophy that I am not very familiar with. It's not quite solipsism, since we seem to have a shared reality with others. That, in itself, causes a bit of confusion.

The LOA cannot reliably account for many things that exist outside of us. I do not believe a person can create a mountain or a river. Nor can a person materialize a fish. The LOA may bring these objects into our lives, but it does not manifest them. The universal mind provides these things for us even before we enter this reality. Our thoughts have no control over these natural structures. God laid the foundation for us. There are certain items afforded to everyone when they come into this world. We are not born into an empty void. The Divine Source provided us with a beautiful planet and abundant resources. In fact, the Divine Source produced the entire universe including the earth, moon, and stars just as the Bible states in Genesis. You could rightly say we had a hand in it, since we are part of the Source. As I suggested previously, the LOA brings the natural world into our lives even though we did not physically manifest it. You may have dreamed of visiting the Grand Canyon when a friend unexpectedly gives you an extra ticket. Our thoughts produced the opportunity, but not the location. I mean, you can't manifest the physical reality of the moon. It already exists for the multitudes. This is a shared resource. It is available to be included in everyone's experience. Societies institute property rights in an effort to define ownership. It works for us to a certain extent. However, the idea of property ownership is just an illusion. We cannot own anything. This notion is difficult to explain since the idea of "possession" is ingrained in our culture. One of the first words we speak is "Mine!"

The LOA asserts that our thoughts create or manifest objects and situations within our sphere of influence. I've often wondered how it's possible for two people to "create" simultaneously. If I create everything I see, and you are creating everything you see, who is responsible for what? I understand this process as a sort of "shared reality." This is a metaphysical term and has a distinct meaning unrelated to other meanings given to it. Let me provide an example. An average woman walking down an ordinary city street decides she wants to buy an orange. Based on that thought, she will definitely manifest the orange released from her mind. As a result, another woman working at a fruit stand is daydreaming about a customer to sell an orange to. Suddenly the realities of these two women merge. Each woman has a specific purpose. In this case, the realities of these two women come together out of both necessity and convenience. There is a mental exchange taking place. An overlapping of realities occurs because of the intent of these women. The supply and demand rule is an excellent example of shared reality. Although it's a complicated matter, it's actually quite easy to visualize. This issue has bugged me for some time. I'm glad it has been resolved.

You may be wondering why some people insist that they want a certain outcome, but end up with something very different. This may be a sign of a situation that is psychological in nature. Here are a couple of possible reasons why someone may sabotage their LOA aspirations. It's possible that an attractionist is not being totally honest with himself or herself about his or her wants and desires. This person may actually be perfectly happy in his or her situation. The attractionist may express the desire to live the high life. In reality, he is completely content living an ordinary middle class lifestyle. Perhaps this confused attractionist is experiencing difficulty using the LOA because he is getting something gratifying out of the constant struggles about which he complains. For example, this person whines about having to go to a job where no one appreciates him. What this person fails to recognize is that he truly enjoys going to his job, because he can complain to others about how terrible it is. He may even get his friends and family to encourage him in carrying on with his disgruntled attitude. Maybe the attention he is getting from his friends and family in some way makes him feel good about himself. People love to be heard. They will even endure pain, both imagined and real, to get a sympathetic ear. Please understand that people aren't so complicated; they just make things appear complicated. It seems to be our nature.

One reason for the LOA's seeming inconsistency comes when a person has made plans before coming into this world. This agenda interferes with what people believe they want to accomplish while they are living out their lives. Reincarnational plans reside in our subconscious, just below our awareness. These plans have to do with the challenges we have set for ourselves in this life. We set specific goals for ourselves in each successive life. There are lessons we must learn. At times, our materialistic motives conflict with our programming. For example, an individual may claim she wants a particular lifestyle, but fails to recognize her innate urge to do something different. Let's pretend that you were a miser in your most recent past life. In your next incarnation, you might choose to be a pauper; perhaps you feel the need to develop an attitude of generosity and gratitude. If this is the case, your pre-life designs will certainly thwart any attempts you make toward building fabulous wealth. The LOA will not help you with your conscious attempts at accumulating riches. You will unknowingly undermine such efforts.

Interestingly, many times our attitudes from our past lives bleed through into this life. Our likes and dislikes often shape our present life to a certain extent. This may even be a deliberate act to test ourselves. It is common for humans to allow the difficulties of a past life to reappear in their next life. It may seem redundant or even irrational, but that is one way to experience the spiritual. Not all of us choose to do it this way. It's just one way to strategize your lesson plan.

I also want to point out that the will of the Universal Mind overrules cosmic law. The Infinite Intelligence implemented the universal laws, and therefore retains the right to override them. This means that the LOA is, in effect, suspended. I am not sure if rule breaking is common practice with the Infinite. You will find that there are times when the cosmic intervenes in your life with good reason. Certain events will unfold regardless of what thought forms your mind is generating. Sometimes we try so hard to accomplish a goal just to find that God has some other project in store for us. We may feel as though we are constantly running into a brick wall with our plans. This is the universal intelligence at work. Our ambitions may not match up with what the cosmic has ordained for our lives. Sometimes we go in one direction and end up in a completely different place. This process can also come from the will of our Greater Self. There are many levels of consciousness that have influence over the direction our lives take. Their intention is always to help us fulfill our highest purpose. We may or may not understand this while going through our tribulations.

Some LOA coaches claim that universal laws are absolute and cannot be interrupted for any reason. I contend that the Infinite works outside of cosmic laws. There are always loopholes and exceptions to the law. Even with the law of gravity, we see that what goes up does not always come down. Aircraft can defy gravity for a certain amount of time. They work within the confines that the Universal Consciousness dictates to accomplish this feat. If we had an independent power source or mechanism, some things would not come down at all. Then there is Jesus who is said to have defied physical laws and walked on water. The Cosmic Architects designed backdoors for their technicians.

These architects or programmers installed laws that work in conjunction with certain physical and universal laws. Some of the relatively unknown laws allow for divine intervention. I do not how often this happens. People often tell me about strange and amazing things that have happened in their lives. These unexplainable events are more than likely instances of divine intervention. My favorite story is the case of the flying baby in Worcester, Massachusetts. As the story goes, an absent-minded father reportedly left his three-month-old son in a car seat on the roof of his car. Lost in his thoughts, the man drove off with his baby still sitting on top. The baby in his car seat rolled off and miraculously landed in the middle of the highway without a scratch. These things happen all of the time. They do not occur because of physical laws; they happen in spite of physical laws.

Law of Expansion

Relax. This law has nothing to do with your waistline. I deem this principle to be of great importance to our spiritual growth. This law mandates that all things must grow.

All conscious entities expand their consciousness both inwards and outwards. Since the multiverse is infinite, there is plenty of room for this. In our own universe, you will notice that things also get bigger. Look at corporations. They always strive for growth in an effort to claim the biggest market share. I can hear you saying, "What about when they go bankrupt?" No problem. The company's resources and personnel will find their way into some other enterprise or empty space. Vacuums exist for only a moment. Spaces are quickly filled. This is a law unto itself. The bottom line is that the principle of expansion requires things to transform in order to grow.

Human consciousness must experience change within each moment to expand. Fortunately, this is inevitable since each unique experience alters our being. Each experience transforms us into a new version of our former selves. These experiences also aid in our expansion. We are collective entities. The information we absorb allows us to gain new insight into the nature of reality and the cosmic truths, since we are part of the whole. There, God also hungers for new experiences. As individuals, we feed "his" appetite through our physical, mental, and emotional activities. There is no end to this process. Expansion is the nature of the Universal Source and all things within it.

Law of Love

I've decided to add one more law. I feel that this one is the most important. It is absolute and immutable, just like the law of mentalism. The LOL (not laugh out loud) is the love emanating from the Divine Source. In fact, it is the Source. This love is spoken of by the most upstanding Christian leaders. It is an unconditional love that takes no notice of human deficiencies. Divine love exists beyond human understanding. It is an experience. A fair number of people have experienced this wonderful sensation. Such an event produces feelings of acceptance, joy, and elation. They result from a union with the Cosmic Mind. A recipient of universal love cannot capture, define, communicate, or explain this experience in any known language.

As you might have guessed, this higher love is not the same as human love, although at times it seems to come close. When we connect to the Source in an intimate way, it changes our perception of the Creator forever. It also changes our beliefs and values. When this truth reveals itself, we realize that we are part of something bigger than ourselves. So now, we can see that the entire universe loves us completely and without reservation. How great is that!

This divine love is infused with consciousness, as is the mental energy that flows out of it. The universal life force holds this world together. Those that practice energy healing cannot successfully do so without directing sincere love to the patient. This is a difficult task for many healers. How many of us honestly love a stranger? In this day and age, when we offer a dollar to a beggar, he may steal our wallet. The Divine Source does not have this fear. As many Christian faiths proclaim, God loves all of us the same. There are no favorites. God holds no grudges; therefore, God has no one to forgive. The angry God comes from Old Testament thinking. The New Testament portrays God as a loving, fatherly figure. Divine love cannot be measured in human terms. There is nothing to compare to it. Everything that is or will ever be was conceived in love through the Cosmic Consciousness. The universe is imbued with it.

Why can't we experience this Godly love in our daily lives? We can, but most of us don't. You see, because we are human, we are somewhat disconnected from the Source. Our amnesia impedes us from knowing the Cosmic's love for us. It has been replaced by a materialistic love of things and for each other. This in itself is a kind of connection to the Divine. We are here, in part, to work on our emotions and advance towards a higher love. The divine love flows through the universe, whether or not we sense it. Love is an innate urge from deep within our being. Although we may deny it, we cannot resist it.

Humans and the Multiverse

The Nature of the Human Spirit

As to the true nature of human beings, you could say that we are denizens of this physical existence. We journey from outer realms to take part in this material reality. We are also multidimensional entities, in that we manifest ourselves in more than one plane at a time. This is possible because we are pure consciousness. This is an extremely difficult concept for most people to grasp.

The first order of business to consider is our soul, or spirit. These two words describe the etheric or astral self, which is simply another body. You could call the astral body a type of energy form, dream body, or light body. Our consciousness inhabits this light body. The astral (light) body is a solid form, except that it is less dense than the physical. The light body is able to take on any appearance you may choose. You might assume the appearance you had when you were in your twenties or thirties. You can take on the form of another person or animal. Your light body can fly, and it can move through solid objects. That's right, just like a ghost. Your light body is the cloak you don immediately following your transition to the other side. A light body is needed to traverse the multiverse, just as you need a physical body to operate in this reality.

My next topic of discussion is the "I am" concept. We identify ourselves as "I am." We have no true names or identifying information. We simply exist. Do you think dogs recognize each other by name? Your precious Prince might know Daisy's name because you have told him enough times, but this is not the natural process one dog uses to identify another. Some people have said dogs do this by smell, but I'm of the opinion that it goes deeper than that. "I am" is something innate to canines that we cannot easily pick up.

When God spoke to Moses from the burning bush, Moses asked for his name to which God replied, "I am that I am." Asking such a question might be akin to asking a bumblebee how he flies. I'm certain bees never stop to think about it. As we accumulate experience, we do take on identities of all kinds, but these are costumes and not who we are. No person has ever been able to put a finger on the nature of consciousness. It is quite elusive. Our individual consciousnesses are part of a greater consciousness. Some refer to this as the Higher Self or Higher Power. I tend to use the term Greater Self, because the word "greater" implies the existence of a much larger entity. This is exactly what we truly are. All of our reincarnational lives comprise this Greater Self, although there is even much more to it than this.

This Higher or Greater Self exists as consciousness. Consciousness is incredibly difficult to comprehend. For one thing, consciousness has no body in a physical, or even energetic sense. It doesn't float invisibly in space either. Consciousness simply exists and is present throughout the multiverse where it resides. Consciousness is awareness. It doesn't even exist as a thought. There really is no description for this unique state. In its pure state, consciousness has no special characteristics to identify it. It can only be recognized by the things it does. Even your energy body is just another vehicle for traversing the many realms of the multiverse. It is difficult to isolate consciousness, because it defies all of the who, what, when, where, how and why questions. In a physical being, consciousness would appear to exist within the person's body. Most people believe it sits in the head. It's true that a part of our consciousness occupies our bodies, but as we are part of the Greater Self, our consciousness also exists in many places at once. In fact, our consciousness exists in many different dimensions across the multiverse. Our consciousness lives many lives, not only in various parts of our planet's history, but also in the timelines of other physical and nonphysical provinces.

Like cellular memory, each "you" retains the memory of each of these past lives. It's like each one of you has a distinct personality and yet all of you think as one. All information gathered becomes part of the collective entity to which each of us is a member. This situation could be likened to the hive mind of bees.

The truth is that we are not special. Even in this reality, a king is the equal of a commoner. Sorry, I hate to be the bringer of bad tidings. We are participating in a real life play. You may be acting as a physician and someone you know may be playing a patient. You may know someone acting out the life of an alcoholic and another soul playing the part of a substance abuse counselor. They are just roles. No one is more important than anyone else. When you are out of your body and on the other side with these people, you will see that we are all the same. In this life, some people have higher status than others. The precious status that we give to one another is particular to the material world. Our designations of honor have no significance in the afterlife. The Greater Self does not play favorites, and neither does the Universal Mind. To some of you this will seem like good news. In that case, I'm glad to be of service.

If you were Alexander the Great in a previous life and shared your enthusiasm with another human or nonhuman entity, he would probably say either "Who cares?" or "So what?" Of course, I'm just making a joke, but there is a real lesson to it. That is – don't take yourself so seriously. Don't get so involved in your various roles that you lose yourself. People get so absorbed in roles that they lose sight of what is important. If the stock market crashes, don't jump off a skyscraper. If your favorite sports team loses, don't shoot yourself. These things are of little consequence to your mission. They may be all-consuming at times, but in the scheme of things, there are bigger things at stake.

One the other hand, these events may be one of the tests you have set up for yourself before entering into life, so you must pay attention to them. Learn from these events, but keep them at arm's length. Do not let anything overtake you. Even those little irritations can draw you in, especially when you think too much.

For the most part, we do not know who we are. Knowledge of the eternal soul is all but hidden from us so that we may carry out our mission. Our true self or consciousness self-evades us entirely. We are left to ponder the deeper mysteries of life in search of answers. Even then, we find ourselves running in circles.

What is the nature of consciousness? Consciousness is awareness of one's existence and outer environment. I assume that without consciousness, the mind could not exist as an independent entity. Therefore, I am sure that consciousness is not merely a function of the mind. It's possible that the mind is a mental vehicle in which consciousness resides. There are ancient philosophies that maintain that consciousness exists wrapped within several layers or bodies. The answer to this question is not so terribly important that we need to lose sleep over it.

Humans define mind or consciousness by those expressions that are easily recognized. This includes all of its mental functions, like emotion, thought, concentration, memory, intellect, and personality traits. These manifestations of consciousness are merely its applications. These mental functions are not consciousness. They are just how we identify it. Many metaphysical practitioners agree with this statement.

Thoughts cannot be identified as the "I am." As I stated before, thoughts are afforded their own awareness. They become agents of the mind after being conceived. Thoughts manifest as objects and events on both the physical and nonphysical planes. Thoughts take on a life of their own, yet they are still part of our consciousness. This is true of all things we create.

The act of fixing our attention on a single object or situation changes the nature of our reality. Our movements from one slice of reality to another may be slight, but perception is relative. The kind of reality we experience looks different every time we change the intensity of our focus. This is similar to the mechanics of dreaming. Since the true nature of reality is hidden from us, we generally do not perceive the alterations that take place as we go about our business. As I explained previously, our minds cycle at different rates, so that our perception of reality takes on a different quality each time we move through it. I'm sure you've hyperfocused on occasion, perhaps while taking a test or some other intense activity. These focus levels are usually in the alpha range. Reality is never static, as the environment we are viewing and manipulating is constantly changing its form. Everything in the universe flows with a rhythm. This includes our consciousness. My hypnosis instructor claims that humans go in and out of hypnosis throughout the day. Hypnosis is a range of focus levels. This includes meditation and daydreaming. Have you ever entered a mild hypnotic state while watching the road when you are driving? What about zoning out when you are vacuuming?

I don't want to get off on a tangent about hypnosis, but since I brought it up, I do want to share one particular encounter related to my experience with it. In my hospice volunteering, I was eager to apply my hypnosis skills to help patients with anxiety, insomnia, and general discomfort. This large hospice organization offers complementary therapy services, such as massage, meditation, pet therapy, music, art, and Reiki. Strangely enough, the volunteer coordinator determined that hypnosis is too controversial to include in their program. It seemed odd to me that she would say this. After spending two months training for this volunteer position, I opted to leave out of frustration. I did go on to give my time to another agency. I also took the time to write a letter to the uninformed volunteer coordinator outlining the facts about hypnosis. This portion of the letter was written as follows:

- Hypnosis is used by physicians and dentists in both pre-operative and post-operative surgery as a form of anesthesia and analgesic.

- No harm can come to patients since they are in complete control of their minds during a hypnosis session. They are free to accept or refuse any suggestion offered by the hypnotherapist. If a patient is not ready to handle certain information, he or she will reject it.

- The hypnotist has no special powers and acts solely as a guide. Hypnotists usually read from scripts that are tailored to suit the patient's needs. Many people use guided imagery in the same manner.

- Hypnosis is nothing more than a state of deep relaxation. It is, in fact, much like meditation.

- Professionally trained hypnotists are certified by respected organizations like the National Guild of Hypnotists.

- Hypnosis was accepted by the American Medical Association as an effective therapy in 1958.

- The Roman Catholic Church gave recognition to hypnosis in 1847 and approved it for childbirth in 1956. This is now known as hypnobirthing.

Try asking a few people what they know about hypnosis. Most will respond that it has something to do with getting in front of an audience and flapping your arms like a chicken. This is stage show hypnosis. It is not representative of clinical hypnosis. There is also the erroneous perception that hypnotists engage in mind control and other unethical practices. Television helped perpetuate this myth. As we become increasingly educated in the nature of the mind, this myth will eventually lose its strength.

Meditation lends itself to some self-hypnosis applications that cross into the psychic realm. One of these applications includes communicating telepathically. How would you like to get inside the mind of your business associate (maybe you wouldn't), your dog, a plant, or anything else that exists? I will assume that everyone would use this information for honorable purposes and not for their own selfish reasons. The following exercise is an excellent technique for connecting to the many entities that make up our reality. It's also useful for learning the secrets of the universe. Follow the instructions in this script:

Human Script

Keep in mind that the level of results you achieve will depend on a number of different factors such as your mood, confidence, health, etc. And don't forget about practice, practice, practice.

Consider the following suggestions:

- Do not engage in strenuous exercise before trying this exercise.

- Stay away from caffeine, stimulating drugs, and alcohol. These chemicals interfere with meditation.

- If you like, you may use soft meditation music.

- Avoid total darkness. Try using dim lighting.

- Make sure your clothes are loose and comfortable

- Lie down on a mat or sit in a comfortable chair

- Do something you might do when you want to relax your body. Do not fall asleep.

- You could look for a good relaxation script on the Internet. There are many styles and choices.

Once you have completely released the tension from your body, take several deep breaths to refresh your body.
Close your eyes and allow your thoughts to slow

down.

You will eventually get to the point where your mind is no longer focused on the outside world.

Your thoughts may feel a bit dreamy.

You may forget where you are. That is fine.

If you are able to focus your thoughts, think of a person you would like to know better. It may be a friend, a co-worker, a relative, or anyone else.

It helps if you have love for this person. It does not have to be the romantic kind of love, just a genuine caring about the well-being of this person helps.

This is true whether or not this person reciprocates your feelings.

Picture this person clearly. See the lines of his face, the shape and color of his eyes. Visualize the person's complexion, the contour of the face, the shape of the mouth. The body style. Clothing. Any other details that will help you to clearly visualize this person. Most people tend to focus on a person's face more than any other part of the body.

What is his characteristic body posture? What is his usual body language? What is his normal tone of voice? All of these identifiers are unique to this person.

Now try to envision this person's personality.

Imagine his overall disposition or attitude. What kind of person is he? What is his mood or temperament? Is this person generally cheerful and pleasant? Is he sad and dejected? Or is he bitter and hostile? Does he possess a sense of humor? Does this person have a nervous personality? Are there any unusual quirks?

These are just some of the character traits a person may have.

What are his habits? Likes and dislikes? It's okay if you don't know.

What are the person's beliefs? If you know.

What kind of intelligence does this person have? Is it academic, emotional, creative, conventional, or some other kind?

When you have identified the predominant traits and emotions of this person, try to use your empathetic side to relate to this person. This sensitivity is the secret to this exercise.

Assume this person's character for a moment.

Allow yourself to be engrossed with his essence.

Your feelings may be very intense, but they will only last as long as you continue this exercise. Remember that you are always in control.

Let your spirit merge with this person.

Feel close to this person.

Feel this person's being.

Based on your knowledge of this person, imagine you are him.

Experience his personality traits that you have envisioned previously.

Become all of those unique qualities that make the person who she is.

Out of this merging, you will begin to know what it is like to be this person.

You will begin to understand his thinking.

You will receive impressions and you may even read his thoughts.

You will experience insights about this person, such as how this person operates.

Things you didn't know about this person will emerge and perhaps you will begin to know this person as well you know yourself.

You may come to know the authentic person behind the face he or she puts on for the world.

The secret behind what makes this person tick will be
    revealed to you.
If your experience with this exercise is successful,
    you may even come to know this person better
    than he knows himself.
Having gained new insights, you can return to the
    common reality fully awake and ready to make use
    of what you have learned.
You might jot down some notes so you can reflect on
    your experience later.

Tree Script

You can obtain the same result from any conscious
entity. The process is slightly different for plants,
animals, and the things we regard as inanimate.
Use the same procedures as previously given to relax your
body and quiet your mind.

Now imagine a tree from your past or one that you
    see in your daily travels. It could be a tree in your yard,
    a special tree in a park, or at some other location that
    has meaning to you. Whatever tree comes to mind is
    special to you because you thought of it. Since this tree
    has some subconscious meaning to you, it should be
    easy for you to connect to its essence.
As you think about this tree, it should create a
    good feeling in you.
In doing this, it may bring up old memories. I'm
    Sure they are good memories.
You may begin to notice a pleasant sense of peace
    and tranquility.
You could also experience a pleasurable sensation.

Allow yourself to be immersed in these feelings.

All the while keep the image of the tree in your
mind.

Imagine the physical characteristics of the tree. The
thick trunk. The rough bark. Its immense size.

Some of these features may apply, depending on
what type of tree you are visualizing.

Think of the unique aspects of this tree.

Feel these characteristics as if they are part of your
own being.

Become the essence of the tree.

Feel as though you are the tree.

Allow yourself to experience what it is like to be this
tree.

Be open to receiving whatever form of mental transmis
sions come to you.

People often disregard thoughts and sensations with
which they do not agree.

Do not interpret, examine, or judge anything you receive
until later.

When you have completed your journey, return to
waking consciousness ready to take notes on what
you have experienced.

I used this method on a tree where I previously lived.
I actually made physical contact with the tree. I do not
know what kind of tree it is. This tree is situated amongst
many other trees. It seemed to stand out from the others. I
was particularly fond of it. When I was able to get into a
quiet space and familiarize myself with the tree, I was surprised to find that it was not focused on the activities of
humans. In my ignorance, I assumed that the tree was interested in our comings and goings. Humans have a tendency to be egocentric. It is our nature to believe that all of

creation is mesmerized by our impressive achievements. This is generally not true of most plant life. Nature is not silently watching us in awe. The exceptions to this are domesticated plants, which form an attachment to their owners. What I did find is that the tree was focused on its relationship with the Universal Consciousness. There were no distinct thoughts. I experienced a feeling. There is no word for this feeling. It was something similar to joy and exhilaration. You could also add reverence and love into the mix. I also experienced a visual representation of the feeling. I could see the tree stretching up toward the sky. The sky was alive. There appeared to be energy between the sky and the tree. This episode lasted only a couple of seconds though the impression was solid. I have gained a new perspective on plants from this experience.

Of course, if you were to offer love to a tree, it would certainly pay attention to your affection. In the early 1970s, the Chipko movement emerged out of India. This movement called for non-violent resistance to tree cutting by surrounding and "hugging" them.[4] Out of this act of mercy came the term "tree hugger." There are now people who go around hugging trees. It's actually common practice in different parts of the world.

Think of the pigeons in the park that crowd around you when you throw them breadcrumbs. They are not the least bit interested in you. They are only interested in the breadcrumbs. The pigeons may become aware of you only briefly when you get too close, just as insects are not con-

---

[4] The Brave Discussion, *Tree Huggers – The Chipko Movement – a story of how a group of women defended their forests by hugging trees,* http://thebravediscussion.com/2011/07/treehuggers-the-chipko-movement-a-story-of-how-a-group-of-women-defended-their-forests-by-hugging-trees, accessed July 28, 2011.

cerned with us until we get in their way. That doesn't include those bugs that see us as food.

My brother raised pigeons in a coop for fun when I was a child. I learned that pigeons are intelligent in human terms and have their own personalities. You see this in the way they interact with each other. They have their own culture, their own dos and don'ts. If you pay close attention, you will see that these birds have their own code of conduct.

Creatures close to our level of consciousness are likely to acknowledge our existence. We like their attention as well. It feeds our ego. Some of these wonderful creatures include dogs, cats, monkeys, whales, dolphins, and other animals we consider to have higher intelligence. We have determined that these creatures are "smart," as they can relate to us, but that has little to do with their behavior towards us. Ask any dog trainer. Other creatures usually do not interact with us the way that we do toward each other. However, that doesn't mean they are any less intelligent than we are. Think about this when you encounter other beings.

The Twilight Zone

As with my commentary on hypnosis, another layer of the consciousness spectrum worth mentioning is an area aptly termed the "twilight zone." This should not be confused with the TV series *Twilight Zone* hosted by Rod Serling. The title of the show may have referred to this important area of the human consciousness, but confuses the matter. I admit that I enjoyed this unusual program when I was a child. The twilight zone is the uncertain point where dreaming and awareness meet. When you are starting to awaken from a nap, or are in a drowsy state before you fall asleep, you will have access to this supernatural window. Bizarre and unexplained occurrences take place in this area of consciousness. Although all five senses can be affected by this altered state, I am most familiar with the visual. "People" and places may appear to you that would otherwise be impossible under normal circumstances.

This is an important area for mystics, shamans, mediums, etc. When these two worlds come together, we see amazing things. The twilight zone is our entry to otherworldly planes of existence. An interaction or exchange takes place between the internal and external environments – the external being the physical reality and the internal being the nonphysical reality. The inner, or invisible, worlds provide us with access to higher knowledge, which may be used to advance our spiritual evolution.

Many, if not all, people have crossed the threshold of the twilight zone. Most quickly brush off their experiences as they awaken or drift off to sleep. Because we are so immersed in physical reality, we dismiss the rare glimpses we are given of the other side. We must have an active awareness to notice these opportunities when they present themselves.

If you do not acknowledge the existence of the twilight zone, then it is effectively shut off to you. Having an open mind makes the ideas in this book possible. That should not be a big surprise. The term *open mind* has more than a superficial or casual meaning. The implications of being open to receive foreign ideas and otherworldly contact goes beyond what I am presenting here. By taking our intense focus off the material world and onto other areas of reality, we allow ourselves to have a balanced experience. I should also mention that I spoke to a prominent medical professional in casual conversation about this subject. I was reassured that it is common to have remarkable visual experiences in the twilight state. Thank goodness for that. If the kind doctor had said otherwise, I might have given up on writing this book.

Phosphenes

When using meditation to obtain assistance from higher beings, one should pay attention to the hypnogogic images that appear in your inner field of vision, known as *phosphenes*. The phosphenes are the images you see when you close your eyes. The phosphenes mark the beginning of your transition from one level of consciousness to an altered state that allows entrance into other worlds. The phosphenes typically appear as simple geometric shapes. They often have color, at least this is what many people report. The phosphenes can look like almost anything. There is no Idiot's Guide to the Afterlife. We rely on the experiences of other people to guide us through it. I might add this book is not a comprehensive operator's manual on the subject either.

If you have trouble seeing the phosphenes, stay in an artificially lit room for five minutes and then turn off the lights (ideally one light) so that the room is completely dark. After shutting the lights off you will see the phosphenes for a few seconds. Now you have an idea as to how they look. Expand your awareness and look for them with your eyes closed. Keep in mind they are always there whether you see them or not. When you are able to visualize them (in a dark room), try opening your eyes for a moment. You will notice that they are still there. Scientists can explain this phenomenon any way they like; it makes no difference. They exist independent of our reality and yet are in it.

As I noted previously, by closing your eyes you automatically relax and enter the lighter cycle. The phosphenes are an indicator of this transition.

Intelligence

Industrialized societies value academic ability above all else. From the time we are children we are taught and tested. This happens over and over. Our parents encouraged us to be superior academians. There is nothing wrong with this as long as we do not neglect other important aspects of our mind, like our emotional and creative intelligence. Tests do very little to measure a person's worth. An intellectually disabled person has far more worth than our superficial judgments we give. They are capable of wonders that have yet to be revealed in this age. I am talking metaphysically of course. Their ability to contribute to society has not been fully realized. The internal mind has greater potential than the external world. Learning is as natural and necessary as breathing. However, we put ourselves in a box by creating tests designed to determine our worth. We have all sorts of personality tests and psychological evaluations. They tell us what kind of person we are and what we are capable of achieving. When we complete any kind of test, we should realize it is only a test, and not an accurate assessment of our character.

If we fall short of being a professional, such as a doctor, engineer, or a lawyer, then we do not measure up to society's standards of excellence. I mean, we all agree that a doctor is more dignified, intelligent, and worthwhile than some department store cashier. Right? Of course not. I'm not saying that a doctor isn't well-versed and capable of performing in his or her area of expertise. You certainly wouldn't want a cashier doing surgery on you. I just think we need to change our attitudes.

As I mentioned previously, I used to be a successful private detective with my own business (I am now retired). When I meet new people, they always ask me what I do, as is the custom in our society. When I respond that I am a retired detective, I always get some variation of, "Oh my God. That sounds exciting. I've always wanted to do that." That kind of attention was a great boost to my ego. It kept me involved in the trade for 20 years. It's nice to have that kind of respect and admiration, however titles have no meaning. Peoples' perceptions of a private investigator are skewed. That's true of a lot of professions.

Being a detective is stimulating at times, but I wouldn't say that it is glamorous or action-packed. People fall for the TV mystique. I enjoyed the early years of my career. When people ask me about it, I tell them this: In my 20s, the work was exciting. In my 30s, it became a job. And when I hit 40, I decided to take early retirement. This is probably true for many in their chosen professions. Because of this, I decided to pursue my calling and undertake a serious study of metaphysics. Detectives investigate the mysteries of the physical world. Metaphysicists explore the great mysteries of the hidden universe. I no longer get the definitive look of wonder from strangers who believe in the mystique of detective drama. I can also say that metaphysics is not quite as lucrative as the investigative profession. There doesn't seem to be a job market for metaphysicists, but it is a rewarding pursuit. Over time, I grew out of my need for others to satisfy my ego. I found that my intense career focus was not conducive to my personal growth and development. Men typically define themselves by their job function. This is unfortunate. There is so much more to life than your job. At the same time, a career can be very rewarding. It doesn't have to be a humanitarian job, either. Actually, people in social services have a high burnout rate. As long as we keep our heads about us, there is no reason why we can't maintain a balanced life. We are certainly capable of that.

Stress

With that last comment, allow me to give my little spiel on stress. We are entities of the Universal Mind entering a foreign land. It can be compared to a good time at our favorite amusement park. We anticipate the excitement of exotic thoughts and emotions that accompany physical existence. We might say to each other before coming into this life, "We're in for a wild ride!" Material reality is a thrilling adventure for otherwise unchallenged entities. Physical life is a special condition that does not typically appear in otherworldly provinces. Because of this, stress is something we willingly and maybe even enthusiastically embrace. God learns through us in our times of stress. As a rule, the perception of stress is always present. If this were not so, we – the Universal Consciousness – would cease to evolve and exist.

This concept may seem a bit "out there," at least to conventional personalities, but as I said before, pieces of this theory have been passed down through countless generations, and can be found throughout present day literature. You may even want to conduct your own research into this. It's important to form your own opinion on such matters. You will find it easier to accept it as true.

Because *we are* the proverbial "supreme being," and a part of all that exists, we have many options available to us. One of our primary mandates is to be fruitful and multiply. Every living and seemingly lifeless being travels in this natural direction. This means that the Universal Mind seeks to grow and evolve. It's stress that makes this possible. This process is very complicated; I can only offer the basics.

Stress is misunderstood. While we think of stress as something to avoid, we fail to see that stress defines us. A friend once told me "the world stretches you." You could imagine this as a rubber band. Left alone with no work to accomplish, the rubber band is all but useless. When we stretch it around an object, the rubber band is now doing something. It is serving its intended purpose. If you do nothing, you learn nothing. On the other hand, if you exert some effort, or work towards some goal, you are likely to improve your life in some way. Therefore, stress is not the bane of existence.

Now I'm not saying that the stressful events we experience can't lead to psychological or even physical harm. One of our challenges is not only to overcome stress, but also to learn from the experience. Understand that stress itself cannot hurt you in any way. That doesn't mean that your reaction to stress can't have a negative effect on your body and your psyche. You may have heard the following statement in a psychology or philosophy class at some point. Objects and situations have no meaning. They only have the meaning we give to them. We interpret and label our experiences. If a big dog bites us, we classify big dogs as being vicious. Our reaction is to stay away from big dogs. If a dog fetches a ball for us, we say it is a good dog and we continue to play with it. In reality, the dog is neither good nor bad. A dog does what is in its nature. Everything else in life is like this. We spend our waking lives forming opinions and making judgments. That is one of the distinct habits of human beings. Therefore, stress does not exist outside of us. We cannot say "my job makes me stressed," or "my kids make me stressed." It is all our doing. That doesn't necessarily make things any easier.

Names

Look at your name. Maybe your name is David Doolittle. How did you get that name? It typically comes from your parents. I hope that you got a good name. Parents can be cruel when it comes to baby names. I knew someone in high school who committed suicide because of the torment he received for his unusual name. Remember, you weren't actually born with your name. That wasn't your name before you came into this world, and it won't be your name in the next world. That's not even your permanent name in this life. You can go to court and legally name change any time you want. In fact, you don't even need to change your name in court. Just start calling yourself Fred Redd. Tell everyone that is your new name. It will catch on. I guarantee it, just as surely as my name is David Almeida.

As you can tell, I have an odd interest in names. As a detective, I had a keen interest in missing persons. Because of this interest, the development of aliases became an area of expertise for me. Please allow me to continue.

In the afterlife, names are not required. Human entities simply recognize each other. We are able to perceive each other's energy. Communication is purely telepathic. Thoughts are easily received as we are able to perceive their vibrations. You needn't worry about identifying your loved ones in the afterlife. You will know them, even if their appearance has changed.

Non-human entities are equally nameless. If you read the Bible, you might recall Moses asking God, as the burning bush, what name "he" goes by. He responded, "I am that I am." Later, this voice from the burning bush became known as Yahweh. As a side note, I believe Yahweh is a non-human entity posing as God. I realize this is a controversial statement. Any time an entity tells you to worship him, you should know that you are dealing with a bothersome non-human entity. They enjoy the attention. They have no power, except the power we give to them. Be on the lookout for these annoying energies. You have better things to do with your life.

The Human Personality

Pertinent to this section is a discussion of the human personality. Each of us has a distinctive character. Most of us recognize each other by our personalities. This is not something that our five senses pick up. It's a function of the sixth sense. Our personality is a part of who we are *in this life*. However, you will find it is something that we carry with us into our other incarnations. Personality is an aspect of our consciousness. There are no suitable descriptive terms for some of the ideas I am trying to relate.

I think that what is most important in regards to the personality is that it is not destroyed in the transition between life and death. I know that we all agree on life after death (or you would not have read this far), but it's nice to know that we retain our personality right into eternity. We do not turn into some mindless, unfeeling part of a larger entity. We retain our individuality.

I know this is true. The first house I lived in had a very aggressive disembodied spirit sharing the space. One evening I was taking a nap. At some point, I became lucid, and suddenly I felt someone or something strike me on the side of my face. The impact didn't hurt me, but I definitely felt it. It made my head spin to the other side, just as it would in physical life. I didn't know what to make of the event, so I went on with business as usual. Then one night my wife was taking a nap and heard mumbling. She said it sounded something like a demonic voice that you would hear in a horror movie. This isn't to say that it *was* a demon voice. That's just how we hear certain spirit voices in physical reality. All my wife was able to take away from this strange occurrence was the name "Keith." We took this to mean that Keith is the entity that hit me. Keith was apparently a human entity who was not happy with us being in his house.

This just shows that we retain our complete personality after the transition. This is true even if we remain in the physical environment. If we believe we are still living out lives, our personality only gets stronger. Once we have moved on to other spheres of existence, we will lose most of those negative traits we have accumulated. When we understand the true nature of physical reality, we will give up the intensity of our pain, grudges, and other nonproductive emotions. For example, if you come across a close relative or friend with whom you had a hostile relationship, you would not be compelled to continue this way. In fact, you are more likely to have a close and loving relationship with that person.

What about us? So how big is consciousness? Is it as big as our bodies? My theory is that consciousness knows no bounds or limitations. It may exist in infinite space or in a single atom. Consciousness can exist in a bodily organ, a house, or even planets. Despite this disparity, no consciousness is bigger than another. In most cases, consciousness can be thought of as the size of an atom. I'll call this concept The Atomic Consciousness Theory.

I propose this theory of mind based on the panpsychic belief that all atoms possess their own consciousness. My impression is that we are no different from any other atom, except we have been given the privilege to experience physical life as humans. This does not mean that other atoms do not enjoy their part in the master plan. For this reason, we should respect all things. Please be considerate of the things you connect with in your journey. We share the road with other travelers.

The Nature of the Other Side

I am in no way a physicist or any kind of physical scientist. I cannot offer any empirical evidence to support the claims put forth in this book. If you have a science background, then you may be able to process this information better than I can. On the other hand, it's fair to say that being a physical scientist can be a hindrance to receiving higher knowledge. The exception to this statement is those scientists that belong to mystical orders.

In early modern times, higher knowledge was imparted to progressive thinkers such as Roger Bacon, Copernicus, Galileo, Columbus, and Magellan who had radical ideas about the world. Humans clearly resist change. They are comfortable being where they are, even if the situation is less than desirable. This attitude slows our progress. Speaking of progress, I would like to give my prediction, that in perhaps three hundred years, the theory of evolution will be disproven. I have a bit of doubt regarding this theory even though it has been firmly implanted in our society by modern science. Please note that spiritual evolution is far different from Darwin's theory.

One model that I can readily agree with is the now discredited steady state universe theory, also called the infinite universe or continuous creation theory. This theory was proposed by Fred Hoyle, Thomas Gold, Hermann Bondi, and others in 1948. This simple theory states that the universe has always existed and continues to expand. This excellent theory is well suited for metaphysics.

The universe is carefully maintained by extra-diemnsional engineers and technicians. What we have is a multi-part effort of the Collective Consciousness to experience its own evolution. The universe was not suddenly blown into existence. As you might guess, I am not a big bang theory enthusiast. Metaphysicists know that the Cosmic seeks to acquire knowledge in order to expand and evolve. That is a prime directive. All things must grow. Just like corporations, the universe gets larger and larger. It learns from our human lives and adds our unique experiences to its infinite databank.

The universe has no beginning and no end. It has always been and will always be. It is truly omnipotent, omniscient, and omnipresent. The alpha and omega. Our physical universe is part of the Universal Consciousness. Everything that can be said of the nonphysical universe also applies to our universe.

The other side is right where you are standing. This is another aspect of time and space. The multiverse is comprised of countless "spheres." These other realities exist right on top of each other. A friend of mine calls this phenomenon "nonlocale." I take this to mean that it is possible to exist nowhere and everywhere at one time. A good analogy is to compare the other side to the internet. If you type into Google "Where is the Internet?," you will receive responses that indicate, "The internet is located nowhere and everywhere." This means that there is no central location for the World Wide Web. Millions of desktop PCs and servers across the globe contribute to the Internet. That is the true nature of the universe.

You can't relate to the dimensional qualities of the other side by saying I am here and you are there. There are no compass points to guide you. There is no up or down. Travel is mental, like everything else in the multiverse. However, you will be thoroughly oriented in hyperspace. If you enter other realities similar to our own after your transition period, you will find that some use the time/space component. Time/space is certainly not unique to our reality. Many other civilizations find time/space useful for getting around. Life without time/space is hard to imagine, because it is all we know.

Suspend your reasoning for a moment, or if that is what you have been all along, then continue to do so. This is the afterlife. It does not correspond to anything we know, except in our dreams, which most of us do not recognize as real. You could actually be standing within several different realities right now (if you stand while you read). There may be buildings and people around you that you do not see. They are most likely unaware of you. They exist at a much higher or lower vibratory rate than you. Our reality is part of the other side, much like a room in a vast hotel. We are separated from other spheres by an imaginary wall, which is simply the way we see reality.

This situation is a real possibility and is even likely. For the most part, the entities in these realities go about their business undisturbed by our own activities. Sometimes you might catch a glimpse of these worlds out of the corner of your eye. You might catch unusual patterns of light or shadows that clue you in. There may be some other circumstance that brings your attention to these realities. If you have a well-developed psyche (reading this book is a good indication of your desire to conquer life's mysteries), you will know when your reality has crossed with another. It will come to you as one of those unexplained happenings. It's a quality that is difficult to relate. Again, you will know it when you see it.

By now, I'm sure you understand that the multiverse holds realities of all kinds. Some realities are noticeably similar to our own. Other realities are inconceivable from our earthly paradigm. Even in one's wildest imagination, these domains are difficult to conceptualize. Neither can their nature be described in any known language. We are limited in our thinking. We have been given only enough information to function in this world. If I say that many of the civilizations that exist on the other side are far more advanced than we are, it is because we are locked into a reality that inhibits our full senses. Even when projecting ourselves into far reaches of the multiverse, we still possess limited thinking. This is also true for our transition. Only sometime after our deaths will we have clarity. At this time, our kind is not concerned with other realities.

An excellent account of one man's journey into the astral world can be found in *Journeys out of the Body* by Robert Monroe. He also wrote two other books entitled *Far Journeys* and *The Ultimate Journey*. You might find these books challenging and even mind boggling. Such is the nature of the afterlife. It seems to have no order to it. There you will find no discernible patterns, reference points, or logical scheme to help you get around. Again, this assumes that you are using your brain to make sense of it.

It is human nature to analyze things. This is one of the many mental processing tools we are given to help us operate in the physical world. Our thinking abilities are particularly useful for this reality. We have been given a special ability to use reasoning to navigate our way through life's complexities. A couple of useful concepts regarding this statement bear mentioning. Linear thinking is a step-by-step problem-solving method. Analytical thinking is a method of separating a subject or situation into its parts in order to study their relationships. These two processing tools are specifically designed for this reality and have no use outside of it. Logic is a tool used to understand one's natural environment. Humans expect the world around them to make sense. When people are subjected to unusual happenings, they are thrown off balance. The supernatural is an example of our rather delicate engineering. Our level of understanding cannot express things outside of our experience. It's safe to say that we cannot analyze God. Logic does not help us understand consciousness, nor does it help define the afterlife. We are slowly moving towards an understanding of these things. The illumination we seek is not earned; it is given. The first step is in our own self-awareness.

Awakenings

What is self-awareness, and why is it important? Self-awareness is defined as being cognizant of one's own personality and uniqueness. This includes feelings, thoughts, behaviors, and other distinct aspects of the self. This definition has limitations. It only works for us at this stage in our development. For purposes of illumination, this definition does little. Self-awareness is the "I am" previously mentioned. It is the realization that you exist as an eternal being. It tells you that you are alive and in many ways invincible. It's the mystical knowledge that you are more than just another brick in the wall or a part of your physical environment. You have the insight to know that you extend beyond the material world. Self-awareness also guides you in the realization that there exists a Greater Self to which you are intimately connected. Along this line of thinking, self-awareness brings us face-to-face with the Collective Consciousness, the creator of all things. This entity is unlike the Gods worshipped by the many religions of the world. These descriptions only begin to describe self-awareness.

Self-awareness is a kind of "psychic awakening." Remember the scene in the first *Matrix* movie (1999) where Neo suddenly awakens in the futuristic pod where he was held captive by the matrix? His world was nothing but an illusion. The operation of reality is similar to this, although the mechanics are quite different.

There is considerable emotion that goes into an awakening. It brings up feelings that a person may never have experienced prior to this. It may bring tears, joy, and excitement. It may also cause a bit of worry or concern. Your new understanding may not generate any particular feeling in you initially; it may hit you later. People often come to this awareness in stages. How it happens…is how it is supposed to happen. There is no right or wrong way to experience it.

The awakening comes in many different ways. It may come from reading certain books. It can come from watching a movie that contains a spiritual message of the kind I am offering in this book. It can happen after attending a lecture, workshop, or seminar on a metaphysical topic. There are many fine preachers of the first truth. In some instances, the awakening is not so obvious and may come disguised in unassuming forms. At other times, the awakening is given to us in scattered signs and symbols. In this instance, we know something incredible is taking place, but we cannot put our finger on it. Awakenings can also happen in the classic "it hit me like a ton of bricks" way. Inspiration is often dramatic.

An awakening is often followed by short or long stretches of inspiration and creativity. This can happen in any area of the human life wheel including family, career, social, physical, and relationships. Sections of the life wheel differ for each person. An illustration of this wheel can be found on the Internet or in many self-help books. Because of our inspiration, new projects may be started in a hurry. Some of them will not be completed, as those flashes of creativity and inspiration can be sporadic in the beginning. All of this is quite normal and does not reflect the individual's reliability.

As you might imagine (especially if you have gone through it), the awakening itself is life changing. I went through mine gradually over a period of years. I knew I was different when I was a child because there were times when I felt outside of the world. I can assure you it's a very common experience. Many intelligent and successful individuals have traveled this road. Later, I began to question reality as each sign presented itself. I knew there was something stirring in those twenty or so years. I cannot explain how your perception changes through the process, but you will definitely see the world differently. I can say with certainty that you will break through the wall that separates us from eternity. The illusion of the material world will be lifted, and the veil before your eyes will be removed. Either immediately or over time, you will notice that things are not what they seem.

Be selective with whom you share your enthusiasm. Not everyone will be as excited as you are. If you choose to disclose your discovery to friends and family, they may think you are insane. Remember, the average Joe is under the spell of physical reality – as he is supposed to be. Humans will cling to their belief in the material world to the very end. It's all they know. These misinformed souls will tell you that if there is anything outside of this universe, it cannot be known.

Awareness

Humans are able to broaden their awareness through meditation. By quieting our minds, we become aware of the sounds, visuals, and other sensations that are normally just like elevator music. Certain styles of meditation work well for this. I am fond of mindfulness meditation – at least for awareness training. Check the internet for books and workshops on the subject.

For those of you who despise meditation, you will be happy to know that there are other methods for increasing your self-awareness. Some people need to move at a faster pace; they like motion. Movement can be relaxing and liberating. It can also bring about great personal insight. The kind of physical disciplines I am most familiar with are yoga, tai chi, and martial arts. When I was a teenager, I practiced an Okinawan karate style called Uechi Ryu. This is "Karate Kid" style (from the popular 1980s film). This system is fairly fast and hard. Karate practices like this one involve maintaining a sweeping awareness of your environment. After studying martial arts for some time, you will develop this valuable awareness. With martial arts awareness, you can almost intuitively anticipate events.

Martial artists are taught to anticipate an attack by an opponent. The martial artist's reflexes are quick and light. At the same time, an accomplished karate practitioner can direct his (or her) chi to deliver a powerful impact to the opponent.

There are times when a martial artist's awareness requires a narrow focus. In this case, the practitioner will direct his energy toward a specific aspect of the opponent or target. The student or master may find it necessary to zero in on something the opponent is doing. It may be the way the person moves or even breathes. For those of you who have seen the first *Star Wars* (which came out in the 1970s), I would like you to recall the scene on the Millennium Falcon where Luke was being trained on the light saber by Obi Wan. Luke was blindfolded with a large helmet as he tried to strike a floating metal ball with his light saber. That is awareness training. I'm sure instructors of gymnastics, boxing, tennis, and other sports have creative methods of teaching awareness.

This same energy of which I have been speaking allows the practitioner's awareness to expand. Tai chi also does this. Yoga is another incredibly powerful practice for developing one's awareness. As you can see, there are many choices available. Some are relatively slow, and some are quite a bit faster.

I will provide a couple of simple methods designed to build your awareness without expending a lot of time and effort. I was employed as a van driver with an ambulance company when I was twenty-one. Part of the initial training involved driver awareness. The trainer had an exercise specifically for this purpose. As you are driving down a busy street, become aware of your surroundings. Whatever you see as you are driving, repeat it out loud. For example:

When you see a green light, say it; "green light."
When you come to a stop sign, say "stop sign."
  If you see a woman crossing the street, say "woman crossing the street."
If it's a kid on a bike riding with the flow of traffic, say "kid on a bike." If you see a dog chasing a cat, say so and hit the brakes. I don't want anyone blaming me.

These are obvious examples. You also want to be aware of the less obvious things you encounter. If you see an unusual parked car, announce it and quickly describe it: "a red Mustang convertible." You may see other vehicles like moving trucks or taxis. If you see businesses, you might name them as well, if there are not too many. You may have to talk quickly. You want to name as many objects as you can that grab your attention. Choose a good location to practice. If you are in Times Square, this can be difficult. Perform this exercise deliberately for fifteen minutes or more. Do this over a period of several days to develop your awareness. Developing a heightened awareness may even make you a safer driver.

Now let's try a different type of awareness training. This experiment deals with the mass-mind. Walk into a busy room. Ensure that there are at least three or more people present. The setting you choose is unimportant: you could choose a small store, an office, a party, a family function, or something similar to these. Above all, it should be inside. You should avoid very large crowds, as the energy is too big to tackle initially. If you are sensitive to emotion, you will have an advantage in this exercise. Upon entering a room, you should move away from the others. Try to keep to yourself for a few moments. Take ten to fifteen seconds to "size up," or "read" the room. To do this, become aware of the emotional content in the room. You are assessing the emotional climate emanating from those present. This is called emotional intuition. You should get a feeling for the collective mood of the people nearby. The general impression you get may be somber or it may be hostile. It may also be joyful or full of fear.

You probably have encountered these emotions in situations like this without even knowing it. Have you ever been in a room that goes silent because one person is about to become confrontational with another, and everyone knows it's coming. Reading a room is similar to this. Again, you are attempting to become aware of the emotional climate of the immediate environment. If you are not a natural at this, it will take a little practice. It will come in time.

Reading the mood of the mass-mind is very useful. It can get you out of some hairy situations. It can even save your life. The ability to sense danger can be developed using this method. At some point, you may find yourself in unfamiliar territory and vulnerable to predators. By using this method, you would be able to sense the presence of unknown persons and their intentions. Those extra seconds you gain may give you the time you need to respond to the enemy. Emotional intuition has helped me this way a number of times. It's a valuable tool for your arsenal. Please give it the consideration it deserves.

OOBEs

For those of you who enjoy the freedom and special knowledge that comes with journeying (projecting), understand that the human entities who maintain this reality frown upon this form of travel. I indicated earlier that our knowledge of the other side is limited while we are alive. According to my literary and spiritual sources, we agree to our amnesia and other special conditions before coming into this life. Life is not something that human spirits are shoved into without support and guidance. We are all part of the master plan.

Out-of-body experiences are infrequent and are not always within our control. These experiences can be scary and upsetting. We do not have an understanding of what we are seeing. The reference points are removed from our conscious memory. People who experience these states report seeing things that are impossible under normal circumstances. The realities that exist are infinite. Every alien creature that we can imagine makes its home here. It defies explanation.

Out-of-body experiences are powerful observations of the other side. Many find themselves in alien environments. There are creatures and beings that may literally look like the ones in movies. I'm thinking of the aliens with the long necks, large heads, and big eyes.

Let me tell you about one of my strange encounters in the nonphysical dimension. It occurred one afternoon when I was sleeping on my sofa in the living room. At some point during my nap, I suddenly found myself standing in front of my body as it lay sleeping. The room had a faint glow. It was similar to night vision. There was one disturbing piece to this out-of-body experience; I saw grasshopper-like creatures sitting on my back. One of the strange creatures was on my back and another was climbing on me. I could see them vividly at the time, though my memory has faded a bit since the event. I took note that these creatures had large, sharp teeth. In fact, that's the first thing I noticed. They also had large lobster claws. I recall the claws being a bit disproportionate to their bodies. I also

remember these large insect creatures having lobster an-
tennae. Most interesting to me was that they were trans-
parent like glass. It also reminded me of white crystal. One
of my theories is that many of the dimensional realities
exist this way. I was staring at one of them for a moment,
and it seemed to look back at me a bit perplexed. I sensed
that these creatures had intelligence, not in a human way,
but they did have more than just awareness. Since I was
frightened by the scene, I was immediately sucked back
into my body. I awoke at once.

I am sure this was not a dream, since I could see
my body and the room around me as I stood there. I know
this is not a compelling story for the skeptics, but it is true.
When something like this happens to you, you know it is
true. I believe these creatures may have been "astral wildlife," as experienced projectionists call them. This means
they are similar to our wildlife. I'm not talking about lions,
tigers, and bears. They are like nothing we have ever seen.
They can't hurt us, as we are beyond the reach of any otherworldly entity. All they can do is scare us.

The 23 Effect

What does the number 23 have to do with the multiverse? Let me begin by giving my own experience with
this unusual number. I encountered the 23 enigma in the
mid-to-late 1990s. I don't recall exactly when and where it
first happened. I do remember it hit me right between the
eyes when I understood that there was some significance
to its appearance in my life. The number appeared everywhere and in the oddest of places. There seemed to be no
rhyme or reason to it. Its appearance never seemed to show
up at a time when something particularly significant was

taking place, or at least I never made a connection. That's not true of other people. I'm sure this experience is quite different for other people. Still, I do know that it is a special number. I'm certain that having an understanding of this unique number is advantageous. I had no idea what it meant at that time. I am still rather puzzled by its appearance in our world.

Some people say that if you look for the number 23, you will find it. That's one answer. There are thousands of people being stalked by 23. What do we make of that? Is it mass hysteria as some medical doctors would conclude? Probably not. In 2007, we saw the release of *The Number 23* starring Jim Carrey and Virginia Madsen. This was about a man driven mad by the 23 enigma. This is a dark movie and appeals to a certain type of moviegoer. Of course, if you are a Jim Carrey fan, you will want to see this film.

The number 23 is a very interesting prime number. It is the number of synchronicities or coincidences. It appears in some of the most unexpected places. Here are some of them:

- There are 23 pairs of chromosomes in human cells
- 23 days in the human biorhythm cycle
- Julius Caesar was stabbed 23 times by Brutus
- The Great Pyramid was erected using 2,300,000 stones
- The Knights Templar had 23 Grand Masters

I am not going to list 23 examples just to be cute. I will let another author do that. There are many famous historical events revolving around the number 23, too numerous to list here. I'm sure you will find them without even trying.

Discordianism is a parody religion started by Mala-clypse the Younger in the years 1958 to 1959. The bible of Discordianism is the *Principia Discordia*. Discordians worship Eris, goddess of chaos. Discordianism asserts that we live in a universe of chaos. This is not just the obvious chaos that we can easily relate to, but also metaphysical chaos that creeps into religion and philosophy. Order is seen by Discordians as an illusion that masks the true nature of our chaotic world. Discordianism is said to be a joke religion that is taken seriously. Discordians make use of humor to perpetuate their philosophies.[5] One interesting belief amongst Discordians is a principle known as the law of fives. Since 2+3=5, those ensnared by the number 23 are subjected to the Law of Fives. The Law of Fives is summarized in the *Principia Discordia* as follows:

- All things happen in fives, or are divisible by or are multiples of five, or are some how directly or indirectly related to 5.

- The law of fives is never wrong.

Discordians fall back on their sense of humor by stating that the more you look for a relationship between the number five and the world at large, the more you are likely to find it. Because of this clever redirection, outsiders to Discordianism accept this reasonable explanation of the Law of Fives.

As far as numerology goes, the Chaldean system states of the number 23:

---

[5] Conservapedia, *Discordianism*, http://www.conservapedia.com/Discordianism, December 29, 2010

"This number is called 'the Royal Star of the Lion.' It is a promise of success, help from superiors and protection from those in high places. In dealing with future events, it is a most fortunate number and a promise of success of one's plans." [6]

I like the sound of that. I'm not sure if I have seen this kind of outstanding success in my own ventures, but I will keep looking for signs.

I believe that the"23 effect" is tied into the architecture of the multiverse. As most physical or metaphysical scientists will tell you, the structure of our universe is based on fantastic mathematical formulas. Numerical equations are the code of the physical universe. Their presence accounts for the minute details of our reality from a waterfall to a ripple on a pond. There is a strong argument for the mathematical universe theory amongst scientists. However, I have no interest in math, so I will not dwell on this point.

The number 23 appears at specific points where infinite realities meet or intersect. We'll call this principle an "angling edge." If you haven't already guessed, I'm not talking about fishing. As I stated previously, etheric spheres do not occupy any space in particular in the multiverse. There is no point of reference to the other side. We are nonlocale. You can instantly go from one place to another. At the same time, there is no point at which the many separate realities of the multiverse do not connect with each other. There are no free-floating spheres of reali-

---

[6] Professional Numerology,

http://www.professionalnumerology.com/chaldeansystem.html, January 3, 2011 ty. These domains do move about, just as our universe is in motion, but they are always connected. The energy that comprises the universe flows back and forth. At times, it may be that two distinct realities meet at a particular point in the physical time/space continuum, triggering a chain of events. When these two domains meet, these realities generate a massive equation, which results in the number 23. These conjunctions put creative forces in motion and account for some of the uncanny events that are characteristic of the number 23. Essentially, the number 23 is the symbolic manifestation of a universal process in which things come together. This numerical representation is not a connotation – good or bad. It is simply an identifier for the metaphysical dynamics at work in this principle. If there is any special meaning being conveyed by the presence of the number 23, it remains unknown.

Symbols

If you have a regular meditation routine or relaxation practice, you may have discovered that otherworldly intelligences use symbols to communicate with us. When you meditate, you open your awareness to other levels of existence. Because of this, you are sure to receive a stream of symbols that you cannot quite make out. It might seem like ticker tape moving very quickly. As you continue meditating, you will eventually see one symbol at a time. Again, you may not be able to grasp the message being conveyed. The Universal Mind may present familiar symbols such as animals, numbers, words, phrases, and even scenes. At least that has been my experience. The symbols may not mean anything to you at the time, or even years later. It can be frustrating trying to figure out what the universe is telling us. Here is a little story that will help you understand the meaning of symbols:

> One day, a curious boy, asked his mother, "What does the cross mean?" Being a devout Christian, the mother replied, "Jesus died on the cross to save us from our sins." As the boy got older, he saw that there were all kinds of crosses in the world. He became fascinated with the Egyptian ankh, Greek cross, Red Cross, Celtic cross, swastika, and others. Each has a different meaning. As the boy grew into a man, he wanted to know the truth: "What does the symbol of the cross really mean? What is the one true interpretation of the cross?" Soon his fascination with crosses became an obsession. He poured through books at the local library and searched for its meaning on the Internet. He consulted his friends and his spiritual teacher. He even asked the old man on the mountain. Still he could not find a satisfactory answer. Upon his death, the man was greeted by the Great Spirit. He posed his burning question to the powerful deity: "What is the meaning of the cross?" The god of his faith looked at him sternly and said, "What does it mean to you?"

I used to try looking up the symbols on the Internet, like the universal dream meaning of a frog or horse. That does little good since the symbols have a specific meaning to the person receiving them. The best thing you can do is keep track of them in a journal. You will want to keep track of any transmissions that appear as signs or symbols, even the ones that come to you in everyday life. You could also keep a dream journal, if you don't already. These are just suggestions. Do what works for you.

In the early 1980s, a superstar performer named Prince entered the pop music scene. You might remember his hits *Little Red Corvette, 1999,* and *Purple Rain,* to name just a few. In 1992, he wrote the Love Symbol Album. With this album, Prince announced that he was changing his name to an unpronounceable symbol. This symbol includes the male and female signs along with the alchemical sign for soapstone. Because the world has no way of identifying him (except on paper, in some cases), the performer is referred to as "The artist formerly known as Prince." You see, we are not capable of relating to others this way. Although our civilization uses symbols on a daily basis, we do not know how to use them effectively.

Most everyone is familiar with the McDonald's logo. What does that mean to you? What do you think of when you see that symbol? It means many things to different people. One person may attach a happy meaning to it (particularly a child); another person, for whatever reason, may be uneasy at the sight of the golden arches. Symbols can have the same effect in the material world as they do in the ethereal realms. As above, so below; as below, so above.

We have not reached a stage where we are able to comprehend the advanced use of symbols. On the other hand, we are able to express ourselves in pictures and paintings, as with Picasso's artwork. We are able to read into it and pull out endless interpretations. That's why art is an advanced form of expression. It's clear from the wall paintings of cave dwellers that they knew the value of symbols. We will eventually reach the point in our development where we have learned to appreciate the true value of symbols.

Senses

I want to mention that each person has a dominant sensory modality. A sensory modality is the way in which we process information. This is how we learn. There are three primary sensory modalities: visual, auditory, and kinesthetic. I am incredibly visual. This is my dominant sensory modality. Auditory is another matter. I must actively listen to what someone is saying to stay on the same page. My wife will attest to that. When a person is giving me directions, my tendency is to visualize what the person is saying. As you can imagine, this just confuses things.

Kinesthetic is another kind of physical sensory perception that many people find valuable and enjoyable. Under some circumstances, human touch is a force for healing. We see this with energy therapies such as Reiki. Gently touching the shoulder of a person in distress can be very comforting.

Physical manipulation of the material world is a requirement for humans; otherwise, we would all be ghosts. Without this tool, we would certainly be handicapped. Determining your sensory modality will help you navigate this reality.

I am intensely aware of other people's emotions. You could say that I am an empath. Empathy is not a recognized modality, but most, if not all, people use it without being aware. It is useful for reading people and helping to connect with them on a deeper level. Incidentally, if you were able to sense all the pain of the world at once, it would overwhelm your being and kill you. Be thankful that we have a built-in mechanism that enables us to block it out. I should also say that there are times when our ability to shut off emotional pain works against us. We have to use our higher senses to be aware of such things without drawing ourselves into other people's terrible circumstances.

There is a term I adopted from a friend who struggles with a severe medical condition that often leaves him unable to engage in normal activities. He calls this state "Being on your back." This is because he has to lie down to get relief from his disabling condition. Being on your back is symbolic of mental, emotional, or physical suffering. We are vulnerable or exposed when we are on our backs. Humans assume this position when surrendering to the universe. This act takes place when all else has failed.

Epilogue

My wife has said to me on many occasions that she isn't concerned with how things work. She only wants to know how to make them work for her. To my wife, the "whys" are irrelevant. She just wants to know the practical applications. This is the general train of thought in conventional reality. Practicality is highly valued in the modern world. There is nothing wrong with that.

There are a small number of people who are curious about the nature of reality. I include myself in that number. We seek answers. The illumined mind is compelled to unlock the secrets of the universe. The mysteries are pursued because the truth is elusive. Some people refer to this as the thrill of the chase. I feel it is a calling. The study of metaphysics is given to passion. It soon becomes one's life work. It does not matter if it is a compensated endeavor or a time-consuming pastime.

This book represents my contribution to the knowledge base of this field of study. I hope to see this pool expand beyond the confines of the mystics. The global mass mind is slowly turning in this direction. The people of the world are beginning to recognize the existence of a spiritual world apart from organized religion. Illumination is becoming attractive to introspective souls. For some, the First Truth is a stepping-stone on this enlightened path.

About the Author

David Almeida is a Board Certified Hypnotist. He is also a Spiritualist and researcher of Rosicrucian philosophy and esoteric knowledge. David was a successful Licensed Private Investigator for over 20 years. His areas of practice included criminal defense, domestic investigations, missing persons, background checks, and fraud. David received the admiration of his corporate and notable clients for his behind the scenes work on their sensitive cases. He completed hundreds of intriguing cases during his distinguished career. David considers himself an "intuitive investigator." He used his uncanny intuitive sense to solve his most difficult cases. While David values his professional experience, he seeks to contribute to the betterment of society by helping others awaken to their true spiritual potential. His curiosity compels him to peer into the unknown searching for lost metaphysical knowledge. David maintains a fulfilling and meaningful life with his wife of 19 years, Galen (a spunky Jack Russell), and Katie (an energetic Labrador Retriever).

Inquiries: davidalmeida@usa.com